Contents

Introduction

In the twenty years I have been working with professional firms worldwide, only two things have remained constant: the first is the ongoing allure of a career in one of these prestigious organisations, and the second is the ridiculous level of pressure anyone embarking on such a career will almost certainly have to endure.

So, while the headlines continue to admonish – 'Can lawyers learn to go home and get more sleep?' was a recent story in the *FT*[1] – the rush of applications for coveted traineeships at law firms, accountancy practices and similar businesses continues each year unabated.

---

1   E Jacobs (2019) 'Can Lawyers Learn To Go Home and Get More Sleep?', *Financial Times*. www.ft.com/content/ac34d02e-9f31-11e9 -9c06-a4640c9feebb

It's not unusual for there to be fifty applications or more for each vacancy in many top firms. The combination of high starting salaries and the promise of varied, intellectually challenging and possibly international opportunities provides further lustre.

But while the big picture remains unchanged, on the ground things are increasingly different. The march of technology has been the single biggest change in the professional landscape. While a mere decade ago, clients might have been willing to wait for an answer, mindful of the limitations of the postal services and the realities of international time zones, the rise of the smartphone means they now expect that answer immediately. Firms used to talk about 24/7 availability as an airy cliché. Now many of their leading practitioners have to live it for real. And while automation has relieved many of today's professionals of the administrative burden of their predecessors, the march of progress has in many ways created more anxiety. If the bots are taking over due diligence today, will they be handling my advisory work tomorrow?

Another key change has been the expectations of the millennial workforce – radically different from those of workers in the past – now dominating the talent pipeline. While this generation is still signing up to professional life in great numbers, they are making it clear that they expect to do so on their own terms. These are people, the research tells us, who don't work for a paycheque; they work for a purpose. They don't want a boss; they want a coach. They are not pursuing job satisfaction; they are pursuing ongoing development. And above all, they are looking for an employer that allows them a good work-life balance and invests in their personal wellbeing.[2] It's safe to say that many professional firms – and in particular their Gen X and Boomer hierarchies – have often viewed these newcomers with a mix of bafflement and irritation. Don't they realise how things have always been done around here? Who the hell do they think they are, anyway? In an ever-raging war for talent, however, even the old behemoths must get with the millennial programme.

One other, and very welcome, change has been the growing willingness to acknowledge that a high-pressure environment carries risks as well as rewards, and the main risk can sometimes be to the psychological wellbeing of the talented individuals who make these firms their healthy profits. When I first started consulting in law firms, it would have been considered a poor career move to openly acknowledge weariness, doubt, anxiety or distress. There was a prevailing 'suck it up' culture – I heard more than one partner respond to news of a junior struggling to cope with the old line 'If you can't stand the heat…' Things are different now. Mental health is slowly getting recognised as being as relevant to a worker's wellbeing as physical health. In the UK, several large firms have signed up

---

2   Gallup (2016) 'How Millennials Want to Live and Work'.
    www.gallup.com/workplace/238073/millennials-work-live.aspx

to a Mindful Business Charter, which has as its specific aim the commitment 'to remove unnecessary sources of workplace stress and promote better mental health and wellbeing' (mindfulbusinesscharter.com).

These contemporary currents conflict with each other to a certain extent and put many firms in a bind. On the one hand, there is a new generation to attend to, in an atmosphere of greater enlightenment about the dangers of exposing individuals to too much pressure too much of the time. And on the other, the new technologies have created a tidal wave of overload which no longer respects time zones, personal space or work-life balance. Something's gotta give – the question is what?

Many of the better firms are slowly adapting their models. New career paths, increased flexibility and 'advanced delivery' models all show some promise in helping young professionals succeed in their chosen careers without sacrificing everything else. But in truth, there is only so much change to be made. These will always remain highly pressurised environments – that is part of their enduring appeal – and as much as the firms must take their duty of care more seriously, the never-ending stream of talented people wanting to forge a sustainable professional career must also take greater responsibility for their own longevity.

I wrote this book because I, too, have experienced the strain of professional life. The travel, the anti-social hours and, in my case, the added insecurity of being essentially a freelance hired help have taken their toll on my own relationships, level of engagement and state of health. Many of the people I have had the privilege of coaching have also been going through their own private torment: often that of the high achiever who no longer feels able to achieve.

One of the lessons I have learned is that health, motivation and confidence are finite resources, and they need careful protection in order to thrive. My aim with this book has been to gather together twenty practical tools and tips which, if applied, and with the support of a genuinely enlightened employer, could help to ensure an individual's precious reserves of psychological, physical and social capital can be protected and optimised for the long term. One of the limitations, in my view, of the way the professions address wellbeing is that their approach is often compartmentalised. Over here is healthy living. Over there is the nebulous concept of resilience. And at the moment, mental health is all over the place. In truth, an individual will need to optimise all of these areas and more if they are to truly thrive in professional life. What follows in this book covers a wide territory and seeks to offer simple, actionable advice in many areas. Sometimes this advice is the direct result of my own experience or that of people I have worked closely with over the years. In other chapters, where I have had the question but not the answer, I have reached out to experts in their respective fields, and I am incredibly grateful for the insights they have allowed me to share.

I have also included four chapters consisting of the transcripts of interviews I carried out with four remarkable people. None of them is a lawyer, an accountant or a consultant. This is quite deliberate. The professional world is introspective, and sometimes it can persuade itself that its pressures are uniquely exacting. We need to get over ourselves. By including the stories of an Olympic athlete, a great stage actor, a polar explorer and a telecoms entrepreneur, I hope to provide some insight and inspiration from quite different fields. These stories remind us that human beings are capable of amazing things, and that many overcome far greater challenges than even the most infuriating client or the most unreasonable deadline.

The twenty optimisation tactics that follow are arranged randomly, but they fall into three broad categories: mind, body and relationships. I suggest you dip in and out of the book, and then identify one tactic from each of the categories that most appeals to you. Use the chart at the back of the book to help you. Once chosen, commit to implementing the three tips every week for three months – and let me know how you get on!

Please visit www.optimise-now.com for bonus resources and news about the Optimise community!

1
The Olympic Athlete: Kristian Thomas

Kristian Thomas was part of the GB men's gymnastics team that won the team Bronze at the London 2012 Olympics. That achievement has to be put in context. No male British gymnast had won an Olympic medal in over one hundred years at that time. The sport had come to be completely dominated by nations such as Russia, Japan and China. To finish on the podium was a remarkable result, and one which brought the men's sport to national prominence in the UK.

Gymnastics is an exceptional sport – its training regime is relentless, the physical demands are extraordinary and until recently its material rewards were meagre. I wanted to get inside the head of an elite gymnast and understand how he manages to keep pushing himself to the limits of endurance year in, year out.

SP: Can you take me into the mindset of that final routine at the London Olympics? What was going through your head when you got to your feet?

KT: So, my very last routine was the floor routine. I was last up, and if I did a clean routine we had a chance. If not, forget it. Four years we'll have to wait to try again.

And I can honestly say, before delivering that routine, I was 100% confident I was going to do it. And I have thought about this so often, trying to think, what are the reasons? And I think part of it is I knew I'd done the numbers in training. I knew I was in good shape.

But I also mentally rehearsed that exact situation in my head for months and months prior to that, not because anyone told me to, but because I thought it would make a difference for me. I had a feeling that I might be the last man up. If we started on pommel and finished on floor, there's a high chance.

And so, I prepared myself in my head, and I'm thinking, okay, what's that going to feel like? What am I going to feel like? What is the competition environment going to feel like? How loud is it going to be in there? And to be honest, by the time that I got to that routine, I was excited to do it. I was 100% confident that I was going to nail that routine, and I was excited to go out there, put my hand up and show everybody what I could do.

Which sounds so strange in probably the most high-pressurised environment I've ever been in, but I could honestly say I was 100% confident doing that, and I do think that mental preparation building up to that routine helped massively for that moment.

SP: And that mental preparation was visualisation, was it?

KT: Pretty much.

And I'd always try and think of pressure as a good thing, knowing how pressure will get the best out of me, not make me crumble. It's going to be something that drives a performance rather than inhibits a performance. And I tried to think about that as well, and process that in my head a little bit. But the thought of, in a few months' time, standing in the corner, presenting, being last man up, deliver a clean routine, we win a medal, that excited me. That made me feel really, really good about myself.

And so, when I got to that moment, I was excited. There was not really much else that I could feel. And then even delivering the routine, generally, as a gymnast, you don't hear anything else going on.

Nine times out of ten, you're in your little zone, swing around the bar, whatever it is, and you won't hear anything. But in that floor routine, doing it, I could hear everything, and it's probably the only time in my career where I've actually felt that. I could hear every tumble, the crowd getting louder and louder and louder, and that gave me even more confidence, as opposed to going, 'God, everybody is watching me.'

Yes, that gave me more confidence to go through the routine. Once I landed the routine, I kind of in my head knew that we had won a medal then, and kind of could just enjoy that moment.

SP: **Are you talking to yourself? Are you saying anything to yourself as this is proceeding?**

KT: Yes. So, during the routine, although you've got milliseconds to make very instinctive decisions: Okay, my feet are in slightly the wrong place here. I need to adjust this. I need to open out slightly earlier. Whatever that might be in the air. But generally, I am talking to myself while I'm doing the routine, most of the time. Okay, calm down. Okay, relax during this. Okay, get my feet in here.

And I also learned that before starting a routine, I just needed to think about one very, very basic thing, something that I knew I could do in my sleep, and that would just get me into the groove of the routine then.

You've done the numbers, so the rest is all muscle memory. It'll fall into place. So, for me, on the floor, it's: Okay, snap my feet on the round off. That's all you need to think about. The rest will happen after that. And then, maybe, throughout the routine, you think, okay, turn in here. Little bits like that, little cues that I rehearsed in my head. Vault. Something as easy as, okay, start my run-up on the right foot. That's all I will think about it. So, if I get that wrong, if I start on my left foot, I've messed up my run-up, I'd have messed everything up then.

SP: **So, that's going through your head, start on the right foot?**

KT: Yes. Start on my right foot and vault. Little things like that that would just be very, very simple cues, nothing for my brain to be too overloaded in that high-pressurised environment, and, yes, that just takes the edge off everything.

SP: Did you ever suffer from nerves?

KT: 100%. I was always nervous. I was always nervous, but I didn't necessarily see that as a bad thing. Obviously, nerves is a way to get the best result out of me.

Once I did get that simple first cue right, as I say, then you relax naturally, and you get into your groove of what you should be doing then. Not all the time. It doesn't happen all the time. Sometimes, nerves get the best of you, and you never relax into your routine.

Parallel bars is the one apparatus [where] I never ever really found those cues to just feel relaxed and composed throughout the routine. I was very twitchy, and that was the nerves. But certain apparatuses, for whatever reason, those cues work for me, and I was able to just compose myself a little bit more and use those nerves as a positive rather than a negative, really.

SP: Okay. So, we've talked about great successes – what about the other side of the coin? At the start of 2013, you had not one, but two injuries. When that second one happened, did anything go through your mind like, well, that's it for this year?

KT: A little bit, to be… Well, to be honest, once I did it, I didn't realise I broke it until a week later. I thought I just hit something hard and it'd be bone bruising. It'll be fine. A week, ten days, I think, went by, and it just wasn't any better at all, so we did go for a scan. Okay, you broke your heel bone. And then

I was like, okay. From there, it was more thinking, okay, the practitioners that helped me rehab my tibia beforehand, they will do a brilliant job in getting me right again.

I need to now work out what I can do on my end to make sure that when I come out of that recovery phase, that I'm ready to go straightaway. For me, I was still in the gym twice a day. I was still working on areas that I knew I could improve on, like the high bar, for example, that wouldn't impact my feet or my legs.

So, I tried to always think about that mindset of: Okay, I can't do this, but where can I make improvements? Probably, that feeling sorry for myself situation, maybe a day, two days max, and then I'd very quickly come around to, okay, I just need to crack on with this now and just...

That's always been part of my DNA. It's probably one of the worst things in the world. I'm not the most sympathetic person. I am very much: come on, you just need to crack on with this, get on with it.

SP: Do you think you're hard on yourself?

KT: I don't think so, to be honest. I think I'm quite reflective. Now I am a little bit older, I'm definitely quite reflective on everything I do. Okay, what was good about that? Where can I make improvements? But I've never seen that as a bad thing, because I also think I know how to switch off when I need to switch off, and I think I've managed to find that balance quite well at the minute.

SP: **So, when things didn't go well, you wouldn't beat yourself up?**

KT: Not necessarily. I almost took it as sort of part and parcel of sport, just that's what happens a little bit as well. You have to expect injuries. You have to expect setbacks along the way. And at the time, I never thought, well, okay, this will only make you stronger, anything like that. It wasn't so much that. It was just, these things happen.

I've seen plenty of athletes before me, after me, that would get injured, and you have to be able to just accept that, move on, and use the other areas to your advantage then. And as I say, for me, I could still be getting better at something else.

To be honest, those injuries were a blessing in disguise to me, because I never actually got back on other apparatuses after those injuries. I just focused on the ones I was better at, and probably had the best four years of my career from 2012 up to 2016. They were a lot more successful than the previous four years, up to winning the Olympic medal.

SP: **I'm really interested in that, because I think wouldn't a lot of people in that situation go: 'Woe is me. I don't have any luck. What on Earth do I have to do?' That narrative in your head of 'this is a disaster' is just not you, is it?**

KT: No, I don't process that way. I never have done. I don't think the people I've been around do either: my parents, my coaches. When something happens, you've got to get on with it. You got to be able to find a way to deal with that.

SP: **To what extent, when you were competing, do you have to be aware of your limitations? Or would you say 'I didn't have any limitations'?**

KT: No. I knew what my limitations were as an athlete, and I knew what I was good at, and how to use that as my strengths, I guess.

SP: **That sounds quite strategic.**

KT: Yes. Definitely. Because I also knew that I wasn't as talented as some of the other guys towards the end of my career, I was the oldest on the team. I knew I couldn't train the same sort of areas. So, I had to rely on certain attributes that I built up throughout my career, and I really pushed those attributes, so people knew what they were. People were aware of them, and I knew one of my best attributes was the fact I could put my hand up under pressure and compete and be consistent. Someone selecting a team, that's exactly what you want.

So, as long as my skill level is relatively up there, might not be the very highest, but it's up there, then that will carry me through for selection to get on to a team. And so, you do. You have to be quite tactful in what your best attributes are, and how you can showcase them. And as I say, I knew I didn't always have the highest difficulty routines on certain pieces, but I knew what my strengths were. I made sure people were aware of those strengths, as an athlete, especially towards the end of my career.

And also, probably worth saying as well, in sport, you are continually surrounded by people that have always got one more medal than you. They've always got something else on top of you. And you become quite aware of that, and you almost can find yourself chasing that next reward, that next accolade, when, actually, if you just do the groundwork first and you think about that process, everything else will just happen.

SP: How disciplined do you have to be about downtime?

KT: I think as I got older, I really realised just how important that was. When I was younger, I'd seen it as more of an opportunity just to go out, see my friends. Didn't really think about what recovery actually was. It was just a day off, a day off from training.

So, I did whatever I wanted, whenever I wanted, on those days off. As I got older and it then became my job, I realised that I had a short space of time, small window to make sure that I recovered properly. I wanted next week's training to be successful, so that meant I had to use whatever recovery process I needed to, whether that's nutrition, sleep, whatever that might look like.

And so, that really then became my day off. That was chill-out day. Might go out for a meal. Might go out to [the] cinema. Other than that, I would try and relax as much as possible. And that became really, really important for me, because it's okay pushing yourself, push yourself, push yourself in the gym, but unless you get the recovery phase right, then you're just going to have a burnout and drop off in performance. So, it's that saying, you can't burn the candle at both ends.

And I also became aware that if I was to have a night out, for example, that would impact the following week's training. So, you just have to be very smart and honest with yourself and think, is this the best situation for me to put myself in? And I'd like to think I was fairly level-headed and, for the most part, got most of that right. I've seen other athletes that perhaps hadn't, and I learnt a little bit from that, and I just knew [within] my own body that that needed to be a recovery day if I was to get back in the gym, push myself the way I needed to the following week.

SP: **I know your coaches have been vital to your success. What does it take to be a great coach?**

KT: The easiest answer for me is coaching the person, not the athlete. And by that I mean, as a good coach, you should be able to adapt your coaching to suit different athletes or different people, because no two people are the same. No two athletes are the same. And general techniques, preps, conditioning will work as a whole. But if you're trying to get the very, very best out of someone, what they do for you is going to be completely different from what they do for me.

So, that coach who has that flexibility and that adaptability to be able to switch between his methods, he's not stuck in one way, his ego doesn't get involved – and that's how it should be – those are the best coaches. And I think if you can do that, then you're already leaps and bounds ahead of most coaches in an elite sport, to be honest.

2
Reframe Adversity Into Opportunity

If I had been Kristian Thomas, my reaction to a serious injury a few months out of the biggest championship of my life would have been quite different. I would have thrown my toys out of my pram, moaned incessantly to anyone who would listen, decided that fate was stacked against me, that I might as well give up, and strop off and sulk somewhere for a few months.

That's why Kristian's response fascinated me so much. He took a potentially devastating event and processed it in the most positive way possible: he thought, 'This gives me an opportunity to build strength and stamina in an event (the high bar) which up until now had been one of my weaker ones. Happy Days!'

This incident is a fantastic example of the mind's ability to play with reality, to interpret it in a variety of ways. It is the embodiment of the famous quote: 'Whether you think you can do something, or whether you think you can't, you're probably right.' While we are powerless to control the stuff that happens to us, good and bad, day in, day out, we absolutely have the power to control our response to it. It seems clear, though, that most of us tend to have a default lens through which we view what happens to us. Mine in the injury scenario (and much else) would be fatalistic – shit happens and we are powerless to do anything about it, so we may as well give up. Kristian's was positive and constructive: how can I make the best of the situation? This default lens (or frame, or 'schema', as the psychologists might call it) is incredibly powerful and is one of the many reasons why Kristian has more Olympic medals than I do!

I have some bad news about this. I'm not a psychologist and I haven't explored this in detail, but the anecdotal evidence of discussing mindset with extraordinary achievers for this book has led me to the conclusion that your family of origin has a lot to do with your capacity to reframe adverse events constructively. Time and again, when people described picking themselves off the floor, dusting themselves down and getting straight back in the game, they would say 'that's the way my parents taught me' or 'that's how it always was in my family growing up'. Now, clearly we can't change our family of origin, but people who were taught from an early age that they have all the resources they need to overcome adversity are at a real advantage when the shit hits the fan in professional life.

For the rest of us, we have to learn to reframe our responses to negative events. It's a hard thing to do because the toxic schema – 'there's nothing you can do when this sort of things happens', 'this proves what you thought all along: you're out of your depth in this place', 'you may as well give up' – can be deeply rooted and, like a favourite song played too often, can be hard to distinguish from background noise. But once your toxic thinking has been identified, it is possible to work on it.

Let me share an example of a junior lawyer who received some fairly harsh feedback from a supervisor on a document she had never worked on before. Now, no one likes harsh feedback, but in a coaching session soon after the event we unpicked what she had told herself about the feedback: 'I'm completely out of my depth here. My supervisor thinks I'm an idiot. No one else gets this sort of feedback. I really doubt whether I'm going to survive in this environment. I'm just not up to it.'

A reframing exercise would take the *opposite* view and would see if the same evidence would fit the new frame:

> I'm relatively new here and have had nothing but good feedback so far. I'm doing fine. The

piece of feedback I have just received was very helpful. This type of work is new to me, and the partner took a lot of time and trouble to show me where I had made mistakes and what to do differently next time. I guess she wouldn't have taken the time to write all those comments if she didn't think I was worth investing in and would get it right next time. I will make sure I absorb the lessons and do it better next time.

The facts are the same; the interpretation is entirely different. Note, though, that this is not a charter for fantasists. The response is not, 'I'm doing great, the feedback was wrong, and I would do the document exactly the same way next time.' Rather, the reframe acknowledges reality and seeks a positive outcome from it.

The real challenge lies in identifying the toxic schema in the first place. Once you have done so, you might be surprised at how often it pops up to offer a one-eyed, incredibly reductive interpretation of your life's events. This is the narrative that needs to be disputed or challenged. Ask yourself, 'Is there another way of looking at this? What are the positives that I am choosing to ignore?'

Ultimately, reframing aids resilience in two ways. It refuses to accept a catastrophic narrative at face value, and it has an abundance view of the personal resources at our disposal to meet a challenge. It is an incredibly powerful tool, as evidenced by the fact that Kristian Thomas enjoyed his most successful year as a gymnast after recovering from serious injury.

KEY QUESTIONS

1. How will this apparently bad event look in a year's time – or five years?
2. What can I learn from this event?
3. What are my options in terms of a positive response to this setback?

3
Refresh To Perform

When British gymnastics became 'professionalised', Kristian Thomas told me that one of the areas the new breed of coaches homed in on was the management of an athlete's downtime.

Any elite sport performance programme will have the same principle at its core. It is axiomatic: you cannot sustain peak performance on the field of play, or the track or in the swimming pool without appropriate rest and recovery. Exactly the same is true of professional life, yet many individuals and some firms believe the axiom does not apply to them. Professional life is awash with stories of repeated 'all-nighters', endless air travel and interminable meetings. Some rail against this ethos and try to build in some recovery time, but plenty more seem intoxicated by the treadmill, in hock to a culture of 'sucking it up'. The consequences are clear. No one can perform at a high level consistently without, in Kristian's words, a 'recovery phase'. Burn out, drop out – or worse – will follow.

There is a sub-set of individuals in professional life who consider themselves 'superheroes'. The normal rules of existence do not apply to them. They wear their Air Miles gold cards like a badge of pride. They are always 'on'. They never say no. Ann Daniels, the polar explorer we will meet in Chapter Seven, identified one particular type of individual as being a liability on an expedition: the alpha male, driving onwards through the snow, heedless of others, sometimes in denial about his own injuries, who ends up being a danger to himself and the rest of the party.

The one inalienable rule of these expeditions, Ann told me, is to pace yourself and never be tempted to skimp on sleep or rest. 'If you exhaust yourself, you're not going to get to the end, you're going to run out. You've got to look after yourself, you've got to be able to perform at all times to the best.'

A lawyer client of mine, Tom, would recognise himself in the 'superhero' stereotype. He was the 'always on' individual in his practice group, destined for great things, driving himself brutally forward in pursuit of partnership. That was until, in the space of six months, his wife left him and he was hospitalised with a heart attack at the age of thirty-two:

> 'Until that point, I had never been forced to stand back from my life, take time out if you like, and actually reflect on what the point of life is and what you really want from it. I was one of those who didn't really take holidays, tended to squirrel myself away in my home office and work weekends, and there was just no quality to my life at all. And the sad thing is, it took a spell in hospital for me to take stock like that. And I think, for people as driven as me, it will always take something as serious as that to knock some sense into them. The more you live your life fantasising about the riches and rewards you will accumulate at some unspecified point in the future, you actually miss the riches and rewards that are around you right now.'

Tom changed his behaviour on medical advice. The rest of us would be wise to do so before getting to that point. There's the obvious stuff like taking our holidays and ensuring most of the weekend is clear for interaction with family and friends. But rest and recovery should be a daily practice too. Addie Pinkster, head of investment firm Adelpha, has some firm advice on this.

> 'Especially if you are a busy woman, let alone have family commitments, get out of yourself!

Stop earlier on the Tube and walk and look up and notice the colours of the leaves and look at the architecture in London, or wherever you are. And look at the roofs and [the] different tiles or window shapes there are. Get out of yourself!'

Many professionals find the transition from 'work' zone to 'home' zone a problematic one. They arrive home still fully in 'work' mode, with all its fractiousness and toxicity. There is a need for a decompression chamber of sorts. Some people I work with use their journey home in the evening to kill two birds with one stone – to get their daily fix of recovery time, and to preserve harmony at home! As Addie suggests, some consciously elongate their journeys home so as to provide some decompression time. Others cycle rather than drive. If they are forced to use public transport, they listen to a mindfulness app or a meditation rather than fretting over the latest email from work. They consciously try to leave the office, the work, behind. And in so doing, they are able to re-engage with family and friends in a positive, less toxic way.

Business often looks wistfully to the world of elite sport for the answers to its most vexing questions. It should learn one of elite sport's most fundamental lessons: there are no gold medals, no world records and no championship wins without the meticulous management of an athlete's recovery time. 'Downtime' isn't a reward for good performance; it is the key to it.

KEY QUESTIONS

1. What practice do you build into your daily routine to help you switch off from work?

2. How do you ensure you manage the transition from work to home without drama?

3. When is your next holiday?

4
Get Moving

Spend time in any central business district in any city in the world, and it will be quite clear that young professionals don't have to be persuaded about the importance of exercise. There will be a plethora of Lycra, squadrons of early-morning runners and a cacophony of music blaring from innumerable gyms and fitness 'zones'.

More senior types also recognise the vital importance of getting out and about when so much of the role is desk-bound, and you will see them snatching an hour here, an hour there, to go to the gym and stagger back to the office – often at the point of exhaustion.

So, the discussion here isn't about the desirability of exercise – most of us know it's essential. The discussion is about what represents *optimised* exercise. With so many professionals being time-pressured, it seems to me very few of us evaluate whether the time we spend exercising is actually doing what we need it to.

I reached out to Elle Linton to get the inside track on optimised fitness. Elle's blog, *Keep it Simpelle*, is one of the most highly regarded in the UK, and she is a fully qualified and in-demand fitness coach. She started the conversation by talking about goals:

> 'It comes down to your goals, and the best way to optimise your training is to focus it on your long-term or short-term goals. If you are looking to lose weight, then cardio is a good option but, actually, weight training is a better option because you end up burning more calories after you exercise. If you're looking to get toned, build more muscle, then cardio is definitely not the route to go; lifting heavier weights is more appropriate.'

I mentioned that time is often used as an excuse for not exercising. I do it myself all the time – 'I'd love to set aside an hour for the gym, but I simply can't find the time…'

Elle was pretty pragmatic:

'One thing I find, personally, is the best way to get your training done is to do it first thing in the morning. I had a comment on a blog post, and someone shared a quote where they said that it's easier to make time at the start of the day, but it's not possible to make extra time at the end of the day. That's a situation I often find myself in, where I've done everything else I wanted to do and the day is done and there's no time left for movement. Also, you don't have to train for 90 minutes. 15 minutes, 10 minutes, 25 minutes is also fine, and more practical in the morning. If you're not a morning person, I personally have been using an app called Fit, which has 25- and 40-minute workouts, and they've been much easier to fit into my schedule. 25 minutes feels like the time it takes to go and make a cup of tea and have a chat with your colleagues, to be honest.'

I wondered about *intensity* in workouts – so many people sign up to classes where the end goal seems to be total exhaustion. Should that be the measure of success?

'I personally wouldn't say so,' Elle told me. She explained:

'If you're in a stressful job as well, I don't think that level of activity and exercise is really going to help you, mentally or physically.

With stressful jobs you're releasing all the stress hormones into your system, and when you're not at work you want to reduce that, so as to help you keep mentally well and keep physically well. Going from that high, and to stay on that high, when you do eventually come down and relax, your body, your immune system, you're likely to get ill and feel low energy, feel down. I would say that it's good to find that balance in your movement and in your exercise where you don't feel shattered at the end of it.'

Nutrition and exercise go hand in hand, and both are notoriously faddish. Elle was sceptical about the current craze for high-protein supplements.

'I feel if you eat a balanced diet, as a nutritionist would tell you, you don't need to supplement, but, realistically, for all of us, including myself, it is hard when you're busy to eat a balanced diet. I would say that you don't need massive levels of protein. You don't have to be downing protein shakes before, during and after your workouts. The main thing when it comes to training and protein is that it's really important to get a balanced snack or meal in within the first 30 minutes of finishing your training session. Sometimes it's easier to get that in a protein shake and that's not a problem, but if you're able to have something else on hand then that's also just as appropriate.'

Above all, Elle was keen to stress the need to integrate exercise into your wider life, rather than keep it to the confines of the gym:

'We spend so much time indoors. Fresh air and space and time to let your mind think about other things other than work and stressful things, it's so important. As a world we're definitely realising more and more that there's more to physical activity than the physical benefit. Mental health is getting a lot more attention these days, so I'm all for getting outdoors, even if it's just a walk. I would also say people should ask themselves about other non-traditional ways of moving that they could fit into their life. Are they able to go for a bike ride with their family on the weekend? Are they able to meet up with their friend for a class or a run rather than drinks? Just are they able to fit exercise or movement into their commute somehow, so that they can kill two birds with one stone?'

KEY QUESTIONS

1. What are your fitness goals?
2. How much time can you realistically set aside for exercise every week?
3. How can you integrate exercise into your wider life?

5
Eliminate Energy Drains

'The sculpture is already complete within the marble block, before I start my work. It is already there, I just have to chisel away the superfluous material.'

This quote, attributed to Michelangelo, has so much to teach us about thriving in professional life. It is not so much addition, but subtraction, which is the key skill. Given that time is our most precious commodity, and that it is finite, we need to ensure we are using every hour effectively. Often, that means we will need to be ruthless at removing the 'superfluous material' in our own lives.

Let's start with *toxic people*. Often, professionals will apply the same perfectionist rigour to their relationships as to their work product. At a junior level, this sometimes manifests as accepting unreasonable behaviour from other people because it is just something they 'ought' to be able to deal with. Then, at a more senior level, when the unreasonable behaviour emanates from peers or juniors, many will go into 'problem-solving' mode. They will treat the other person as a project to get stuck into – they will give them endless second chances and try and adapt their own approach to indulge the other person, mainly because they are conflict-averse but also because they have it in mind that this is a problem they ought to be able to 'fix'.

There is a real danger in spending too much time indulging the poor behaviour of other people. If, in the famous phrase attributed to Jim Rohn, you are the average of the five people you spend most time with, there can be something profoundly damaging about having your own confidence, motivation and morale chipped away by one or two 'energy drains', be they colleagues or clients.

What to do? More senior professionals are often in the happy position of choosing who they work with; those at the start of their careers are not so blessed. But you can limit the amount of time you spend socialising with toxic people. Or be proactive about asking to work with someone else. Or simply refuse to get drawn into gossip, back-biting or bitching. Toxic people hate nothing more than being ignored.

You also need to eliminate *unhelpful ways of thinking*. This is sometimes challenging, as they can be deep-seated, and a coach or therapist may be required to help you identify them. Nevertheless, one thing I have noticed about all the top performers I interviewed for this book is that their mental models tend to be very constructive. Their models support their endeavours rather than sabotage or undermine them. There are several examples in this book of the kind of mental models adopted by these people. If you can, get some space between you and your habitual thought patterns, hold them up for examination and ask how useful each one really is. Is it helping you get through the day? Is it creating confidence or anxiety? Eliminate the negative and replace it with the positive, which sounds ludicrously glib but will take effort – in my case, several years of therapy!

No examination of what we could strip out of our lives would be complete without considering the mixed blessing of *the internet and social media* in our lives. There seems to be scientific consensus that addiction to our devices is real, and damaging.[3] If you feel that some of the time you spend surfing or browsing could be better spent interacting with real people, there is a whole digital detox movement with plenty of tips for you just waiting to be discovered online!

But seriously…turning off your notifications would be a start. Set limits on your screen time by using the feature that most smart phones have for this purpose.

---

3   J De-Sola Gutiérrez, F Rodríguez de Fonseca and G Rubio, 'Cell-Phone Addiction: A Review', *Frontiers in Psychiatry* 7:175. https://doi.org/10.3389/fpsyt.2016.00175

Only access apps or social media at specific points in the day. Remove your mobile phone from the bedroom. Go 'greyscale' on your phone to make the screen less enticing. All these are examples of tips to combat the way our devices have encroached upon our lives. Again, it is a question of efficacy: does the time you spend online or onscreen help or hinder your mission in life? Be ruthless with anything that hinders.

There is one other concept that could usefully be chiselled away from many professional's lives: *busyness*. This is the notion that only by demonstrating just how busy you are do you communicate your full sense of value. One of my clients, Julie, describes how she overcame this pernicious state of mind:

> 'When I started here I got caught up in the
> whole "presenteeism" thing, that you had to
> be seen to be busy, busy, busy all the time to
> demonstrate your worth. People even used to
> brag about the number of meetings they would
> be in that day, or how many emails would be
> in their inbox in the time it took them to go to
> the loo. There was this connection being made
> between being frenetic and being effective. But
> then I started working in a team led by the
> most brilliant manager of my career who said,
> "You are all intelligent people, and I will judge
> you by your output, not your input. Deliver
> what you need to deliver in the most efficient
> way possible – which means prioritising the

highest-value actions every morning and saying no to everything else." And that's pretty much been my secret of success in this place – the ability to distinguish between actions and practices that get me where I want to go and those that are a distraction and just waste time. You have to be able to manage your diary and realise that a lot of the stuff people spend their time ostentatiously doing is pointless fluff.'

KEY QUESTIONS

1. How many toxic people are there in your life?

2. How aware are you of the time you spend online? How much of that time is well spent?

3. How much of what you did today was for show – ie, not helping you achieve a specific objective? How can you limit that kind of activity going forward?

6
Put Boundaries Around 'Keystone' Relationships

'The thing I hate most about this job is that I'm constantly having to cancel arrangements with my friends.'

'I try to get home to see the kids before bedtime, but often it's just not possible.'

'I get all the stuff about business development and nurturing client relationships, and I'd love to just catch up with people and go for a drink, but I honestly don't get the time.'

When I hear these kinds of comments – which I do all the time – I'm put in mind of the cartoon character who saws through the branch of a tree only to remember he's standing on it. As he hurtles to the ground there's a dumb look on his face that conveys something like, 'Why didn't I think this through?'

Just as toxic relationships can have a catastrophic effect on our quality of life, positive ones are the key to health and happiness. The relationships within that close circle of friends and family I refer to as 'keystone' relationships – because a keystone is the piece of the arch that holds the entire structure in place and allows it to bear weight: without it, you are left with a pile of rubble on the floor.

Certainly, professional life takes its toll on relationships. The hours are unforgiving and the pressure is often intense. But for every broken marriage and strained friendship I hear about, there are plenty more marriages that thrive and friendships that endure. What's the difference? It doesn't come down to the old canard of time. Everyone has the same 168 hours a week. It's the way we choose to spend them and prioritise them that can vary radically.

The ability to set boundaries to protect these keystone relationships, and the willingness to engage in difficult conversations to police them, in my experience is a strong predictor of a successful professional. The trouble is, often the need for the boundary is only recognised in retrospect, and too late.

Paul, whose comments follow, is a partner at a real estate consultancy.

> 'I think in the early part of your career you
> accept the trade-off, that the hours are going

to be unsociable and that there may be some impact on your home life. But it's big money and good prospects and I think you turn a blind eye to that. I think where I went wrong was in being indiscriminate – I became known in the team as the guy who was willing to do the client socialising, do the travelling, I made my name on the back of that to be honest, and you create a monster that can never be satiated. People are contacting you all the time to do this, do that, and at first you are flattered and in career terms it can be very beneficial. But it comes at a cost, and for me the cost was in my marriage. I don't think I read the warning signs there at all; I was so up my own arse and intoxicated with work that it was only when we had split up and I was unpacking the boxes in my rented flat that I thought – wait a minute. Just what are you are doing the work for? What sort of a life are you left with?'

The key is to identify those keystone relationships you need to protect, and ensure your colleagues and clients are aware of their importance to you so they are not surprised or disappointed when from time to time you prioritise those people over work. The challenge I often get to this is, 'You don't know my clients.' Then educate them. The difficulty comes, as in Paul's case, when you set up an expectation that – quite reasonably – the client then expects you to meet.

There is a wider point here than simply preserving your relationships with those closest to you. Professional life, despite the march of technology and the predictions that we will all be automated out of existence in the next decade or so, is still predicated on relationships. Make sure there is time in your diary to reach out to people: old clients, new acquaintances, people you meet in passing. Above all, try to look for and celebrate other peoples' achievements and successes. The 'father' of positive psychology, Martin Seligman, has something interesting to say in his book *Flourish* about the importance of these kinds of touchpoints:

> 'How you celebrate with someone is more predictive of strong relations than how you fight. People often tell us about a victory, a triumph or some less momentous good thing that happens to them. How we respond can either build the relationship or undermine it.'[4]

So watch out for, and respond to, those achievement notifications on LinkedIn. Read the firm newsletter. Create a spreadsheet of people in your wider network (or download one for free at www.optimise-now.com) and make a note of when you last contacted them, and when you will next do so. Build some time into your calendar at least weekly to simply catch up with people.

---

4   M Seligman, *Flourish: A new understanding of happiness and well-being – and how to achieve them* (Simon & Schuster, 2011)

Ringfence this time as if it were hours to be billed to your most important client.

Remembering to be proactive about relationships, and the time spent nurturing them, can seem a bit of a chore. It can easily slip off your to-do list in favour of chargeable work or something with a more immediate return on your investment of time. But it is in fact the best investment you can make. No man is an island; and no professional sustains a long-term career ship-wrecked and alone in the midst of an unforgiving sea.

KEY QUESTIONS

1. Have I identified my 'keystone' relationships?
2. Do I have systems and boundaries in place to protect my time with those people?
3. Do I have calendar time booked out each week to nurture less critical but still important second-tier relationships?

7
The Polar Explorer: Ann Daniels

Ann Daniels was working in a bank in the north of England when she answered an ad that was to change her life. The ad invited applications to join an all-women expedition to the North Pole, and, by beating off the competition from 200-odd women during a rigorous selection process on Dartmoor, Ann made the team. The expedition was successful, and it ignited her passion for polar adventure. Together with teammate Caroline Hamilton, she became the first British woman in history to reach both the North and the South poles as part of an all-female team, and Ann has since returned to both poles on numerous occasions as an expedition leader.

SP: **What comes to mind when you think 'that was tough'?**

AD: The 2002 expedition.[5] After 37 days we had only gone 69 of the 500 miles. We've got frostbite, the terrain is moving back almost faster than we could walk.

SP: **How did you do it?**

AD: We just have to survive today and keep going today. So, we have to get up, get out the tent, do our breaks. And how can we add a little bit more? We could do five minutes extra per session. Just five minutes extra, and by doing five minutes extra, it potentially didn't make much difference to the amount of mileage you're going to do in five minutes. But what it did was it meant we were giving our best. Therefore, we were in control of what we were doing. Couldn't control the environment, but we were doing everything we could do and always doing that little bit more to make it possible. And that's, I think, a key to everything.

SP: **I like that. And in that situation, is it the mind or the body that starts to fail first?**

AD: Your body fails first and then your mind's got to... You have to fight your mind all the time and it's your mind that's in control. If you do not get your right mindset, you're not going to make it. Doesn't matter how strong you are. I have seen stronger people than me in the Arctic. I've led stronger people than me physically, but if they haven't got their mind in the right place, it affects the whole body and how they perform.

---

5   Expedition to the North Pole with two team members, Pom Oliver and Caroline Hamilton

SP: **So, when you say mindset, what do you mean?**

AD: So, if we talk about when I take people on an expedition, they are out of their comfort zone completely. So, they might not be that cold when they've got the right clothing on, they're pulling a sledge. But they're in an unknown situation, and therefore they start to panic a bit because it's cold, we're not going fast enough, we can't do that. And you can almost see the panic. They're feeling that they're not able to do it. I can't do this, this is too difficult, that means they don't do it. And you can get them around.

Pack your sledge, that's all you have to do. And then we have to ski forward and we'll add another 2 minutes, and then you look at the positives of it.

So, yes, it is cold, and yes, the environment's moving, but how far have we gone? Oh, we've gone half a mile. And then look at the other things that you can pull in.

SP: **So, the body can start to fail, but if you've got the mindset you can overcome that?**

AD: You can overcome it. I'll tell you about an incident that happened in the South Pole. This is about your mind. Pom and I would do the cooking across from each other, so we brought all the pans, we did everything. My job was to maintain the cookers – they fail a lot in the cold, the rings don't work, they leak. So, I was always responsible for maintaining the cookers, putting them together when they didn't work.

So, one day we're cooking and then Pom got up to do something, I cannot remember what. The pan of water was just boiling, and she kicked it over my foot. The whole pan went on the floor, the cookers went out because there's water on them all. We hadn't eaten at all. We'd just had a long day and the pain [in] my foot was huge. So, I just put my foot out of the tent. We had a vestibule, it wasn't out in the tundra, it was in the vestibule. I just thought, this is too bad for me to deal with and I've got to deal with this emergency situation because I'm the one who knows the cookers.

Somebody went, 'Oh, let's just go to bed.' I went, 'No we have to eat, we have to get those cookers alight, we've got to do that.' So, I dried them all off. I just kept my foot outside, dried them all off. I put the pain in another box, dried them all off, got it all sorted, got them alight, put the water back on and the emergency was over.

So, then I thought, 'Right, I'm going to bring my foot in and it's all over, now I can cry,' because it was so painful. So, I brought my foot in, and I was just about to burst into tears because the pain was overwhelming my whole body. I looked at Pom and Pom had done it. She was in a world of pain and I thought, you can't cry.

You cannot cry because look, it's worse for her having done it, and I knew that, so I just couldn't and didn't. I gave my foot to Zoe and she looked at it and it hit the ten o'clock news. My foot. The blister was huge. And so she dressed it and we went, 'What are we going to do?' You can't ski on it, what am I going to do? And then Zoe came up with the idea.

She cut the hole in the matting around the blister and then glued two or three of the ridge rests together so that when my boot was on the mat, it went on the mat and never touched the blister, so I could ski.

But coming back to your mindset, that is how strong your mind is. God, I wanted to cry. I just had to put it in a box because I knew it was an emergency situation. I could have very easily just given in to it and gone, 'Oh, look at what you've done,' and failed, and then nobody else would have lit the cookers because they would have all been panicking about me. They'd have taken my lead.

If they'd been looking after me the situation wouldn't have been dealt with. And the only thing that got it sorted was that I was able to not have a go at Pom, or not start sobbing and just keep hold of myself. When we skied the next day I just knew it was still in me and I had to let it out, and so there's a big distance and there's wind, nobody could tell, and I just sobbed it out and nobody was there and that was fine.

SP: **In those really stressful situations, do you see a difference in the way men respond and women respond?**

AD: Yes and no. I think men do respond differently, but I can't say better or worse.

I think where men are different to women is that men are more conditioned to not ask for help, to feel they can do it, to go at it in a more physical way. My looking at all the men I've worked with, they will help a female to the ends of the earth, it's in their DNA, but they can't ask for help for themselves, it's an obstacle.

SP: I think that's fascinating. Even in the extreme situations you're talking about, they won't ask for help?

AD: In the extreme, they find it tough to ask for help. That's wrong.

SP: So, when it's the three of you women, the way the three of you communicate with each other, is that very different?

AD: Yes, it's very different. It's very different. We talk a lot. We're happy to check each other. We're always watching each other for either frostbite or what have you. If we're having a down day in as much as sometimes you are going to have a down day when everything's hell, and your sledge is too heavy, then we will happily go, 'I'm just having a tough day.' 'Right, well let me just take one of your bags,' and we'll happily hand it over. Do extra work.

SP: And how honest do you have to be about your own personal resources, limitations. What I mean by that is: is a way of getting where you wanted to go the recognition that sometimes you do need to take it a bit easier? Or is it all about no, we've just got to drive on, we've got to keep at it?

AD: No, you have to rest and recover. You have to be honest if you're having a tough day. I find it difficult. I do. I know that's one of my really difficult things, and so I have conversations with myself about – well, you just have to say, 'I'm finding it tough.' But, what I do when I'm planning... See, a lot is in the planning.

When I'm planning something, I will plan on it to succeed rather than fail. So, you have to eat, you have to drink. So, I will set in a rigid 'we will ski for an hour and a half'. It might be an hour and 20.

I look at the team and think right, we'll start at an hour and 20 because it's a new team. And at an hour and 20, I will check my watch and I will stop the team. Right, now we need to eat, we need to drink, and we need to check our fingers, our toes, our clothes; if you need to go [to] the loo, go now. So those are also the rules.

SP: **But what about the other way around? If someone says actually let's forget about the break and just let's just keep going. Stuff the hour and 20, let's do two hours?**

AD: No. Don't do that. Never.

If, let's say, in the morning we're all doing really well, and we want to add, I don't add to the skiing sessions because you might add 5 or 10 minutes and then you're slowing down and you're absolutely shattered at the end of the night. So, we will never add at the start of the day.

At the end of the day we will say, do you know what, we feel fine, let's do another 20 minutes. That I will do. And then we can have a conversation because you do get stronger. Okay, we're doing really well, perhaps we can do more. Right, well let's change it for an hour and 30 for today and then that day you try and do a bit more because we do look at doing more, but I don't change on the foot because you don't know what you'll be like at the end of the day. You've got to look at the whole team, and also you've got to look at the big picture.

And never stop and not eat. And if you exhaust yourself, you're not going to get to the end, you're going to run out. You've got to look after yourself, you've got to be able to perform at all times to the best.

I took two guys for training once when we were putting an expedition together, and what I did with them was – I was a bit scared because they had a lot of experience – and I said, 'Right, I'm going to watch you for day one.' And I said, 'This is what we're going to do, but it's you two, you're the team, I'm just helping you. We're going to ski for an hour and 15 and then you'll stop. You'll take it in turns at the front, but all I'm going to do is observe you.'

And they went all day. And at the end of the day, God, I thought I was going to die, I could hardly keep up. But I did, and at the end, one of them dropped, he could hardly put the tent up. So, we sat. I let them do it, I didn't stop them because it was a training trip, and we got in and we talked about it and I said, 'Right, we need to talk about what happened,' and then I wasn't scared anymore because I knew what I could add to their team.

'You didn't eat properly, so by the end of the day, you were hypoglycaemic. You didn't really stop. You went for three hours. You never looked back to see if your friend was all right.'

So, we talked about it all and I said, 'You're a team, and you want to laugh, you want to stop, you want to enjoy.' So, the next day I went, 'I'm going to lead this.' And I did the whole day. And I said, 'I'm just going to put in everything I've said we have to do, and I will check, and chat.' And we stopped, and we had a laugh and then we carried on.

We went further. We had a really good time just by building the breaks in, and I said, 'It's not checking on a mate because he's weaker; you're a team member.' At the end, we did that day and then they took over again, and they went, 'That was just so amazing to watch each other.' And it's just my experience; I know not to push people and it works better. I want to enjoy it. I don't want to have a crap time.

8
Track Progress As Well As Results

How often do you end the working day in frustration, settling down on the sofa with a gnawing sense that nothing significant has been *achieved* that day? If our work is to be meaningful – and all the science suggests that it must be if we are to feel fully engaged – then surely a sense of achievement is a precondition?[6] Days without achievement can play into a powerful narrative of being in the wrong job, or not being good

6   S Achor et al (2018) '9 Out of 10 People Are Willing to Earn Less Money to Do More-Meaningful Work', *Harvard Business Review*. https://hbr.org/2018/11/9-out-of-10-people-are-willing-to-earn-less -money-to-do-more-meaningful-work

enough at the one we are in, and pretty soon our whole professional identity can come unstuck.

I noticed something interesting about several of the people I interviewed for this book: they were often engaged in extraordinary endeavours. Reaching one or other of the poles for Ann Daniels. Committing the part of King Lear to memory for Sir Antony Sher. Winning an Olympic medal for Kristian Thomas. Any of these objectives could easily instil overwhelm and the paralysis or capitulation that often results from it. Contrary to the oft-heard advice to begin with the end in mind, these top performers largely ignored the end goal. It was too big, too likely to intimidate or distract. Instead, they would find a unit of progress that was manageable and repeatable and concentrate on that. The poles were reached in 15-minute intervals where the progress was measured in terms of putting one foot in front of the other during those intervals. King Lear was learned one line at a time – and the achievement was in putting together enough lines that a whole speech was mastered. And Kristian's journey to the Olympics was measured in training sessions – an increase in stamina on one piece of apparatus, say, almost but not quite imperceptible from his effort the day before.

Progress towards a goal is how goals are achieved. But my experience with many professionals is that progress – incremental progress – often goes unnoticed and unrewarded. We want the 'big win'. We want the client to be so blown away by our work product that our bosses take immediate notice and fast-track us for promotion. We want our junior staff to return a delegated piece of work to us 100% right, first time. We want our office to be turning a healthy profit and retaining all its key staff and smashing the competition. And, indeed, if we fixate on what the management guru Jim Collins used to term the 'Big Hairy Audacious Goals',[7] progress can seem impossibly slow, and no wonder we slump on the sofa some nights thinking, 'What the hell is the point?'

The key is to focus attention on process as opposed to results. Famously, the comedian Jerry Seinfeld gave some advice to Brad Isaac, an aspiring stand-up comic who asked for some tips on getting on in a hugely competitive business. Isaac recalled:

> 'He said the way to be a better comic was to create better jokes and the way to create better jokes was to write every day. He told me to get a big wall calendar that has a whole year on one page and hang it on a prominent wall. The next step was to get a big red magic marker. He said for each day that I do my task of writing, I get to put a big red X over that day. After a few days you'll have a chain. Just keep at it and the chain will grow longer every day.

---

7   J C Collins and J I Porras, *Built To Last: Successful habits of visionary companies* (HarperBusiness, 1994)

You'll like seeing that chain, especially when
you get a few weeks under your belt. Your
only job is to not break the chain.'[8]

Identify a process that if repeated, like writing jokes
every day for a comedian, will bring you closer to your
goal. Maybe you make a point of proactively sharing
knowledge about the way a particular client likes to
operate across your whole team, and you notice the
client gradually move more and more work your firm's
way. You keep delegating and patiently providing
feedback, and you'll notice the gradual improvement
in the work product you receive back from your juniors.
You schedule a catch-up coffee once a week with a
different contact in your network, and you notice an
increase in the number of referrals you start to receive.
The input drives the output, and the key is consistent
application of effort, day in, day out.

Once the *process* has been identified, you need a way of
tracking *progress*, and there are many options to choose
from. There are apps that allow you to note your own
progress on a daily basis; you can call a meeting with
your team once a week where the aim is to acknowledge
what progress was made in the last week as well as
identify upcoming challenges for the week ahead; and
in addition to a daily to-do list where things are crossed
off when they are completed, why not initiate a daily

---

8   G Trapani (2007) 'Jerry Seinfeld's Productivity Secret', Lifehacker.com.
     https://lifehacker.com/jerry-seinfelds-productivity-secret-281626

'have done' list that sets out all the positive steps you have taken to move incrementally towards a given goal? (Download our version at www.optimise-now.com)

If we measure our own success solely by the achievement of major goals, we will by definition have to wait a long time to celebrate. We will be reminded on a daily basis of what we do not have and how far away we are from our set goal. It's a debilitating state of mind. By turning attention to input and incremental progress, we can recognise the progress we make on a daily basis and the discipline we have learned to apply. And as Ann Daniels' expeditions illustrate, she didn't reach the North Pole by wishful thinking, or by beating herself up, but by putting one ski in front of the other, day after day.

KEY QUESTIONS

1. What is better about this week than the last?
2. What action am I committing to on a daily basis?
3. What system do I have in place to help me track my progress?

9
Get Comfortable Disappointing People

I caught up with a friend of mine recently who I hadn't seen in a while.

'How are things?' I asked.

She rolled her eyes and slumped in her chair.

> 'I've been in back-to-back meetings all day. I've just spent an hour and a half doing my emails. I had a really difficult feedback conversation at lunchtime with one of the new hires. I'm absolutely shattered. And the worst of it is, I don't feel like I've actually got anything done today.'

She said she felt 'under water' all the time, never achieving much in the day but always feeling frantically busy.

Her problem is one I see in many professionals: she's too nice. Too eager to please. She has mistakenly confused 'pleasing everyone' with 'professionalism'. It is a sure-fire way to ensure low productivity, rising panic and a sense of overwhelm.

Here's the thing. We all have the same 1,440 minutes in a day. Productive people don't suddenly acquire an extra 250 minutes more than the rest of us. They recognise that time is a finite commodity but that the demands on them in professional life are infinite, so something's gotta give.

There are fundamentally only three options with any task or request that comes our way. We can do it. We can get someone else to do it. Or we can (politely) decline it. People who are continually 'under water' have 'do it' as their default. Effective, optimised people have no problem declining requests that have little relevance to the key tasks they wish to accomplish. Their time, as the most precious commodity of all, is strictly boundaried.

Email, of course, is the biggest threat to real productivity, because it often contains other peoples' ideas about how we should spend our time. The most optimised people I know treat it as the insidious enemy it is: they check it between 9am and 10am and again between 4pm and 5pm, but otherwise not at all, knowing that buys them six hours in between of productive worktime.

Cal Newport, and his range of books starting with *Deep Work*, has done as much as anyone to draw attention to the productivity deficit in today's tech-saturated world. He makes the point that, for the vast majority of us, two to three hours a day is all we can muster for what he calls 'deep work' – that full-beam, brain-aching, value-maxing labour that is genuinely transformational and justifies our fat fees. The rest is mere admin.

In order to be genuinely productive, we need to find out when we tend to be most 'on it' – are we early birds or night owls? – and protect that time like a tigress would her cubs. Newport – who, like me, is at his best in the morning (this entire book was written between the hours of 9am and 11am, without distraction from other people on pain of death) – advocates the splendidly titled Monk Mode Morning.[9] For his most productive periods of time, he puts a fence around those hours and ensures there is no distraction. No calls. No emails. No meetings. To anyone who asks about his availability for the following day, the reply is simple: 'Try me after noon.' You may say this is impractical – but even if you manage to carve out a Monk Mode Morning once a week or once a fortnight, you will be taking a step to optimise your chance of doing 'deep work'.

---

9   C Newport, *Deep Work: Rules for focused success in a distracted world* (Grand Central Publishing, 2016)

The same discipline is needed with meetings. Everyone knows the majority of meetings are a waste of time: poorly facilitated, meandering and often with no clear outcomes. But people still seem unwilling to hit 'decline' when the next invite arrives in their inbox. Why? Question the need to attend every meeting. Only call one when there are clear deliverables that need to be achieved. And employ the technique of one of my clients, who mandated that the 'standard meeting unit of time' for his team should be decreased from one hour to 40 minutes. The result? More was achieved because nearly two and a half hours a day were freed up for every member of his team to do some work rather than talk about doing it.

Imagine the hours that make up your working day were real estate – your garden, say, or that nice sunny terrace where you like to have a coffee in the summertime. How accommodating would you be if one of your neighbours decided to drive their motorhome right into the middle of it, and stayed there all day, belching out equal quantities of diesel fumes and Led Zeppelin? That's pretty much what is happening every time you unthinkingly accept another meeting invitation, spend time wading through an email which has little relevance to you other than the fact that you were cc'd, or indulge another interruption when you're trying to crank out that important document.

Optimisation is about knowing what is important, creating conditions where what is important can be nurtured, and weeding out the rest. This has a slightly unpleasant corollary: letting other people know they cannot expect to squat on your most productive time is a conversation you need to be comfortable having, over and over until they get the message. And if this is not possible with certain senior people, or for large tracts of your day, then make sure you can carve out at least a couple of hours a day for that deep work.

And it is not always other people you need to disappoint. Resisting that urge to check the news, check Facebook or otherwise fritter away time in a wholly non-productive way could give you back an hour or so every day to do something more useful.

KEY QUESTIONS

1. Which meetings could I usefully decline?
2. What would I have to do to secure 'monk mode' time?
3. Can I limit my access to email and social media to three or four fixed times in the day?

10
Find A Safe Space For Critical Reflection

Work. Eat. Sleep. Work. Eat. Sleep. Repeat.

One of the characteristics of modern professional life is that it is relentless. You can be so immersed in the development of your career that there is no means to gain any perspective on it. But the unexamined life, as Socrates apparently said, is worthless. How, then, to build in some time for reflection?

It is interesting that in the 'caring professions' – healthcare, social work, even teaching – the concept of critical reflection is built into the system. As a key text on building resilience in social work puts it:

'Managing emotionally charged situations and dealing with uncertainty and complexity are intrinsic to the social work role. It is therefore important for social workers to recognize and address the "not knowing" elements of practice, and the fear and anxiety that this can evoke, in order to protect their wellbeing and maintain optimum job performance. The source of negative emotions such as fear and anxiety may not necessarily be recognized or managed effectively by the social worker, however, which can impair their job performance and lead to stress and burnout. Based on the early writings of Schön (1983) and subsequent research across the helping professions, critical reflection has emerged as an important learning tool to help employees manage complexity and ambiguity and cope effectively with situations where a straightforward technical solution cannot be found.'[10]

Dealing with uncertainty and complexity is as much a key to working successfully in a professional service firm as it is in social work – but how many trainee lawyers or accountants are encouraged to embrace critical reflection as a coping mechanism? And I would suggest even fewer can call upon the formal structures of supervision available to those in the caring professions – and

---

10   L Grant and G Kinman (eds) *Developing Resilience in Social Workers* (Red Globe Press, 2014)

indeed are compelled to engage with – throughout their professional lives.

Journaling is one way of introducing some reflective time into your day or week. One lawyer I spoke with puts it like this:

> 'I try and find time every week to write in my journal. It's not just random observations of what has happened; I really try and recall the stuff that has gone well or some comment that someone made to me that made me feel good. I write down the things I feel grateful for, and try and keep a track of the good stuff that is happening, because I think you can get so lost under the weight of the work – and for me it's particularly bad in the winter – that you can feel demoralised if you're not careful.'

This approach happens to have a sound base of evidence behind it. *Appreciative enquiry* is a well-established mode of reflection that concentrates on what is working rather than on what is not. It was developed in the 1980s, when David Cooperrider and Suresh Srivastva at Case Western Reserve University sought to challenge the traditional approach to problem-solving in the organisational setting.[11] Rather than coming at

---

11 D L Cooperrider, S Srivastva (1987) 'Appreciative Inquiry in Organizational life', published in *Research in Organizational Change And Development. Vol. 1.* (eds R W Woodman and W A Pasmore) (JAI Press, 1987)

every issue as if it were a problem, and seeking first to identify flaws and failings, what would happen if we tried to isolate what is working and build from there?

Using the appreciative enquiry approach to writing a journal entry would involve recalling a recent event or experience that went well, understanding the skills and talents you deployed to bring that positive event about, and considering how you might apply that same set of skills more widely to replicate it more often. There are two important aspects to this process: it forces us to focus on what has gone *well* in our immediate past, when our predisposition may be to only recognise errors; and it is ultimately future-focused – it lets us dare to dream about a positive future.

Another approach to critical reflection involves the analysis of a so-called 'critical incident'. This can be done alone with a journal but is best approached in a small group (ideally between three and five people) of trusted colleagues. Ideally these would be close peers – the process can be less successful if line supervisors are involved. I have known a small group of colleagues to meet very effectively like this every few weeks to provide a 'safe space' for critical reflection. The session tends to be 45 minutes in length, and the exact process varies, but generally one person will bring an issue to the group and they will become the 'lead' for that session only. The lead will outline something that happened in their professional life that they are unsure or concerned about. The purpose of the others in the group is to listen attentively; they should not provide pat solutions ('why didn't you just…?' 'I would have just…') but rather ask the sort of open questions that encourage the lead to work through alternatives and options that he/she may not have considered:

- 'How did you prepare for this?'
- 'What other resources were available?'
- 'What were you assuming?'
- 'How exactly did you phrase the request?'
- 'What makes you so sure about what the client thought?'

The above are all examples of open questions that encourage the lead to reflect, perhaps for the first time, on the way they went about the task. This process goes on until the lead wants it to stop, and ideally they will summarise what they have learned and identify some options they could try should the same situation recur.

I am convinced that professionals are missing a trick by not building some sort of critical reflection into their working week. It is an opportunity to analyse and consider their own practice in the light of the collective experience of their peers. It is not unusual to find individuals walking away from such a session encouraged, not just because they have found the answers but because they realised they were not alone in finding a particular situation challenging.

KEY QUESTIONS

1. When did you last keep a diary?

2. What was the best thing that happened to you today?

3. Which three or four colleagues would be open to starting a 'learning pod'?

11

Get Feedback And Adjust Course

'I think it's very important to have a feedback loop, where you're constantly thinking about what you've done and how you could be doing it better. I think that's the single best piece of advice: constantly think about how you could be doing things better and questioning yourself.'
— Elon Musk

I can't say I've had much direct personal experience of extreme sports, but I enjoy the vicarious thrill of watching films about those who excel at them. Two of the best are *Jeremy Jones' Deeper*, on the subject of snowboarding, and *Free Solo*, which documents Alex Honnold's terrifying climb of El Capitan without ropes in 2017. While both of these films induce the kind of cold-sweat fear that Hollywood franchises can only dream about, I find there is something mesmerising about the artistry of the protagonists. Watching Honnold gingerly assess the sheer rock face at 3,000 feet in the air, moving vegetation aside with his fingers to slowly perfect his hold, is to watch someone in tune with his environment like no other. Likewise, for Jeremy Jones hurtling down the side of mountains:

> 'The snow is so deep you need to use your arms and chest to swim, and your legs to ride. It also collapses underfoot, so you're riding mini avalanches and dodging slough slides…you can't see below. Or to the side. Every time the midline is crossed, it's a leap into the abyss.'[12]

Like everyone else who watches these feats of daring, I ponder how these people have cheated death. Of course, luck plays a part, and long may their luck continue. But there is also something to be said for deep expertise – the kind of expertise that pays microscopic attention to action, reaction and instantaneous adjustments. The feel of the snow, the graze of the rock. A recognition that a failure to respond to tiny changes in the environment could mean certain death.

In less arduous situations, in our daily working lives, our ability to thrive is likewise dependent on our ability to measure our impact and adjust course if that impact

---

12   Quoted in S Kotler, *The Rise of Superman: Decoding the science of ultimate human performance* (New Harvest, 2014)

is sub-optimal. Neither part of this process – the getting of the feedback and then the acting on it – is easy.

What process do you have in place at the moment for gathering feedback on your own performance? If you are lucky, you might get a ten-minute chat every month or so with your line manager. More likely, you will be still stuck with the dreaded annual 'appraisal', which can so easily become a bureaucratic box-ticking exercise of little value to the manager or the managed. Managing performance effectively, in real time, is one of those holy grails in organisational development that seems as elusive now as it was twenty years ago.

Nevertheless, getting timely feedback is imperative, and if your firm does not provide the means of getting it from your superiors you are left with two options: establish your own system or buy in external help. Your own system might simply involve getting into the habit of asking the question, 'How can I execute better?' This question is infinitely preferable to 'How did I do?' with its undertone of insecurity and desire for reassurance. If you ask, 'How can I execute this task/process/interaction better?' you are forcing the other person to think critically and give you the kind of feedback which will enable course correction.

'Buying in' will generally mean engaging the services of an external coach. In my totally biased opinion – I have spent a good deal of my career on coaching assignments – these can be extremely valuable but only if your coach fulfils one vital criterion. *They must be willing to tell you in plain language the things about yourself you don't want to hear.* If you finish a coaching session feeling uplifted and comfortable, you have chosen the wrong coach. As Daniel Kahneman, the Nobel-winning psychologist, puts it, the most valuable voice you must ensure you get to hear is the dissenting one.[13] A coaching session should be uncomfortable. You need to be brought face to face with your deficiencies, held accountable for your failure to act or adapt, and be motivated to leave the session and make the necessary changes.

In my experience – and I know I am probably saying goodbye to a lucrative revenue stream by saying so – the 'making the necessary changes' bit is incredibly rare. Even if we find a coach who is prepared to give us the unvarnished truth, most of us find putting the lesson into action tough. It's as if Alex Honnold's fingers kept telling him that the rock face was crumbling but he continued to clutch forcefully at it anyway.

The problem, of course, lies in the pain we experience with cognitive dissonance. We find holding two contradictory viewpoints uncomfortable, so our brains seem programmed to revert to the safety of the comfort zone and ignore the evidence that suggests we were wrong,

13 D Kahneman, 'Episode 68: Putting Your Intuition on Ice, The Knowledge Project' [podcast], 12 October 2019. https://fs.blog/knowledge-project/daniel-kahneman

misguided or in need of a change in direction. I can tell you you are over-committed and that you need to start declining more meetings. It's a hard lesson to put into practice. If you can do it, you'll be in the company of greatness – Warren Buffett's sidekick Charlie Munger often likes to relate this observation about Charles Darwin:

'[Darwin's success] was due in large measure to his working method, which violated all my rules for misery and particularly emphasized a backward twist in that he always gave priority attention to evidence tending to disconfirm whatever cherished and hard-won theory he already had. In contrast, most people early achieve and later intensify a tendency to process new and disconfirming information so that any original conclusion remains intact.'[14]

KEY QUESTIONS

1. What system do you have in place for receiving regular feedback about your performance?
2. Can you give an example of, within the last three months, adapting your behaviour as a result of feedback?
3. Which of your closely held beliefs do you regularly review and update?

---

14   Harvard School Commencement Address, June 13 1986

12
Be Alert To Wilful Blindness

I was as cynical as the next person about all this 'be your best self' guff. It sounds too airy, too wishy-washy, to offer much of value to the day-to-day grind of professional life. Then I had the pleasure of talking to people who had thrived in exceptional circumstances, such as the Arctic and the battlefields of Iraq and Afghanistan, in the course of my research for this book. A common thread running through those conversations has made me think differently about homing in on the positive stuff because, in those extreme environments, being fully aware of your own strengths isn't just feel-good, it's about survival.

In such situations, the management of resources becomes absolutely crucial. Ann Daniels in the Antarctic knew that one of her strengths was the management of the cooking equipment – and that knowledge ensured her expedition team didn't go hungry, even when she was in excruciating pain after the accident with the boiling water. She was clear about her strength and her responsibility, and she did what was required. Kristian Thomas, towards the end of his career as a gymnast, knew that his strengths were consistency and performing under pressure – and those were the things he delivered for the team.

If we continue to deny our own strengths, or overlook them, we are not being agreeably self-deprecating or modest; we become a liability because an optimised team is one in which everyone is clear about their roles and executes relentlessly. But the psychology of many high-performing professionals is such that they don't get to first base: unless you are clear about your own strengths, how can you make your fullest contribution?

'Wilful blindness' has a specific definition in law. It describes a situation in which someone deliberately ignores information that may make them liable if it became public knowledge. I use the term in a different way. I use it to describe people who refuse to acknowledge their own strengths and spend most of their time focusing on their weaknesses. This meaning is connected with the perfectionist mindset so common among high-performing professionals: the tendency to default to the flaw, the problem, the deficit, and ignore the strength, the solution, the abundance. It's a sad fact that many people simply lose sight of what makes them unique, and it often requires real effort to dismantle the accumulated layers of doubt, denial and denunciation that conceal the hidden truth within: here are my strengths, and here is the basis of my contribution to my team, my organisation and the world at large.

For Jungian psychologists, accessing the 'inner child' is often helpful if we seem to have lost sight of where our strengths lie. Jung himself, at a pivotal moment of his career, found reconnecting with his childhood self, who played passionately with building blocks and created model villages, enlightening. 'The small boy is still around,' he said, 'and possesses a creative life which I lack.' From that point until the end of his days, he would make time to sit at his home on the shores of Lake Zurich building castles in the sand. He was connecting with the creative part of himself and, in so doing, enabling thoughts and patterns to emerge which he subsequently used in his writing.[15]

Sometimes, fatigue gets in the way of acknowledging your strengths. A medical consultant I interviewed was acutely aware of this:

---

15 C G Jung and A Jaffé, *Memories, Dreams, Reflections* (Fontana Press, 1963)

'I think, when you're tired and stressed and have maybe done lots of late shifts or whatever, it is very easy to start getting sucked into a "glass half empty" mentality. You know: the system is shit, my bosses are shit, I'm shit. There's this cycle of negativity. And often all it takes is a few good nights' sleep, or an afternoon doing something completely unconnected with work, to realise that I am doing good stuff, I've maybe improved several people's lives in the past week, and that there's light as well as shade.'

Addie Pinkster is a former City banker who went on to found Adelpha, a female-led investor network. She sees a gender aspect to this issue:

'It's amazing how successful women find it difficult to announce themselves properly. I will work with them on that. So, if someone walks in, I'll let them introduce themselves once. But if they undersell themselves, I will just stop the meeting, take them outside and say, "That's not a great way to introduce yourself. You are this. This is who you are in my eyes. I'm going to write these ten words down for you and the next time you can read it off the piece of paper."

It is a case of affirmation and directness. I'll give you an example: we had a brilliant

investor come in yesterday; she hasn't worked
in six years, having had children. But her
background was brilliant. She's a prolific
investor. She's an incredibly successful investor,
but in her mind she has no place anymore in
a corporate environment. It had taken about
three months to drag her into the room. She
still didn't think she would be credible.

So I said, "It's very simple: you've done twenty
years on hedge funds, you're a compliance
expert and you're a private investor. And,
by the way, that's the modest version. There
aren't many other people in here who've made
£12 million in the last three years in private
investments, let alone had two babies." I
had to give her this script, she'd say it three
or four times and then hopefully she started
believing it.'

In the absence of an adviser like Addie, we need to
write that script for ourselves. And to make that script
credible, we need to start noticing all the good stuff
that happens every day that our professional minds
tend to be blind to.

Addie again:

'What I personally do is I write down, in the
back of my day book, anything positive that
someone says to me that actually resonates;

I write it down so that it's near to hand for the next time I'm not feeling that great. There was a consultant we had in for a while and she used to turn to me after a meeting and go, "That was f****** amazing, Addie. Do you have any idea how good that was?" She made me notice the things that I wasn't noticing myself. And we need to continually remind ourselves of our strengths, to get that embedded in our brains.'

KEY QUESTIONS

1. What used to absorb you as a child, and how can you revisit it as an adult?

2. Where do you record your daily/weekly achievements?

3. How do you introduce yourself in a way that highlights your accomplishments?

13
The Actor: Sir Antony Sher

Is any profession more precarious than acting? There are endless rejections, and then, even when successful, the actor stands vulnerable before the unforgiving gaze of the spotlight, the audience and the critics. You need a special kind of resilience to survive in that business. Sir Antony Sher grew up in South Africa, a shy, artistic child at odds with the country's apartheid-era culture. He crossed the world at the age of nineteen to audition to train as an actor in London, where he was rejected by RADA with the warning that not only was he not good enough for the country's most esteemed drama school but he should abandon all hope of a career on the stage and go do something different. He didn't. Instead, he became one of the greatest stage actors of his generation. Many respected critics would say that his performances as Richard III and Macbeth were definitive. He is also an accomplished artist and writer, having published several gripping diaries which illuminate the journey he goes on to bring his landmark performances to the stage. I spoke to him just after he had completed a long run in the role many call the actor's Everest, King Lear.

SP: So, was Lear a Mount Everest to climb when you played him?

AS: No. I suppose my discovery was that it isn't that different from the other great Shakespeare parts. Each of them is absolutely enormous. Each of them feels like Everest in different ways. And you come to each of them with a sense of inadequacy and humility – and excitement, of course. How am I going to do this iconic part? And Lear really wasn't that different, although I'd been warned that it was. Of course, it takes an enormous amount of experience, I guess, to play it. And of course, it's got some formidable challenges, primarily the storm scene. You've basically got a man arguing with a storm. And just vocally, and hard for the director, how to create that image? It's a huge challenge. But, otherwise, it was as exhilarating and punishing as them all. I can't really detect a difference now.

SP: Tell me about Lear's ear.[16]

AS: Well, I think that the body will invent strange reasons for you not to do this task that is difficult to do.

---

16   Sher was afflicted with a mysterious ear condition as he rehearsed the role, which almost led to him withdrawing from the production

SP: So, it was psychosomatic?

AS: I still can't tell. It's hard to believe that it wasn't, because it just came upon me so conveniently. But I think, if I think back over my career, there've been different [times] when I've had different things happen to me that seems to be…

SP: Such as? Which other ones?

AS: The worst was actual stage fright, which I suffered from for about two years. This was around about the time I was doing Othello. And then carried on through several shows. And was cured, oddly enough, by doing a one-man show, the play about Primo Levi.

SP: So, I think many people will find that astonishing. Stage fright for a professional actor? How did it manifest itself? Would it strike when you were on stage or before you were going on?

AS: On the stage. It's a very curious thing. You're saying the lines. You can be saying the lines and thinking of something else. Actors do that all the time. But I'd be saying the lines and one voice in my head would start saying, 'You're going to dry. You're going to fuck up.'

So, that's going on while you're speaking. And then, another voice would be telling the first voice to shut up. So, you'd have this voice: 'You're going to dry.' You'd have this other voice: 'Shut up. Go away.'

And there'd be me in the middle. And it really got to times when other actors who were playing the scenes with me would describe me going pale and starting to sweat. But it never broke down completely. They noticed, and I felt these phases of the performance where I'd be beset by this thing.

But the curious thing I think about stage fright is that it's actually waking up to the reality of what you're actually doing. We weren't built to stand in front of 1,000 people, having learnt this enormous, complicated classical text. And to speak it for three hours, as the centre of attention. So, in a way, stage fright is simply saying, 'What's going on here? Look at all those people looking at you!'

SP: **But it's not helpful.**

AS: It's not. No.

SP: **So, the way you dealt with it was by saying, 'Hang it, I'm going to do a one-man show and beat this thing.'**

AS: Because there's nowhere to hide with a one-man show. And by the one-man show being about such an important subject as Auschwitz, the Holocaust, you just have to have a respect to that and to the terrors that Primo Levi himself… That are on such a different scale to the terror of stage fright, that you're embarrassed to even have the condition, because it's inappropriate to what you're describing in the piece.

SP: **So, that must have felt like a huge challenge, no? To walk out on stage with the whole evening before you, and only you on stage for company.**

AS: It was. And made it from many points of view one of the most special experiences of my life. Not just my career, but my life. Just learning in that detail about that period of history.

SP: **You say several times in your diaries that you love a challenge. I'd really like you, if you can, to shed a bit of light on the time when you arrived in London, in 1968,**

aged nineteen, expecting the greatest drama schools to welcome you with open arms. And, of course, they don't. And you get that savage rejection from RADA, that says, 'Not only are we not accepting you, we strongly advise a different career.' If I'd received that at nineteen, it would have completely crushed me. And I would have taken their advice and gone and done something different. You didn't. You're miles from home. You're on the other side of the world. You've had savage rejection. What made you carry on?

AS: It's really very simple. It was my mother. It really is as simple as that. Because I would have given up. I really didn't have huge confidence in myself. And I was still at that stage very uncertain about whether I really [wanted] to be an actor. I had for so long planned to go to art school.

And that was going to be my future; then, this acting thing had come along and I was going with it. But I wasn't sure. And I could easily have been thrown off course, but my mother had that certainty just as a character. She had a certainty, which I lack. And it was something about her saying, 'They're wrong. They are wrong.'

SP: So, it's a pushy mother we all need. Is that the secret to success?

AS: In my case, yes!

SP: You went on, of course, to star in many productions, and you have published several diaries about the rehearsal process. You seem very vulnerable as you are developing a role. How does it work with the director? How does the director offer you feedback that is helpful, without strangling the part before it is really born?

AS: Two things. One, if it was one of the really big parts, you'll have had a lot of discussions with them before you started.

SP: So, you're aligned from the beginning?

AS: Yes. And you'd have to share some creative decisions, particularly nowadays where you could set a Shakespeare on the deck of the Titanic, or whatever. You'd have to be in agreement that you were prepared to do that kind of Shakespeare. But then, in rehearsals, if they're a director you trust, their feedback will be invaluable. Absolutely terrific. I love notes. I love getting feedback. I love the director saying, 'that doesn't work', or 'that could work', or whatever. And in the earlier days, Terry Hands was a great teacher of how to perform the classics.[17] For me, coming from a background that had no theatre in it, or certainly no classical theatre, my entire time at the RSC has really been a learning process. And Terry was a fabulous teacher. I remember thinking in the early years, 'I'm being paid to get these master classes from these leading world experts in Shakespeare. I should be paying them.'

SP: So, you'd be open to it. You'd drink in that feedback.

AS: Yes.

---

17   Artistic Director, Royal Shakespeare Company, 1978–1994

SP: Is there a point when opening night is moving into view, when actually it needs to close down? When, 'Now I'd like it to be set and actually I don't want to tinker with it anymore'? Or, are you tinkering with it the whole time?

AS: A good production, a good performance, won't be set in stone on opening night, but will carry on. And you'll often find six months into a run with a great play, you'll understand how to do things. And you'll think, 'If only I'd known this when we were opening.'

So, there is a great voyage of discovery that really never ends. But, of course, opening night, which is a completely false structure really, does put a pressure on. And you've just got to learn different ways of how to deal with that.

David Tennant's got a phrase I like very much. It's about panic management. And David, who seems the coolest guy in the world, you suddenly have a picture of him in his dressing room, which I certainly know from my own experience, of having to talk to yourself. Reach yourself and find a way of calming, of being able to go down those steps to stand in the wings, and then step out.

SP: So, do you have a ritual? Is there a process you always go through leading up to the moment you step on stage?

AS: Yes. I come in much earlier than other people and do a private warm-up, preferably on stage, but otherwise in a rehearsal room. Which will be physical, vocal, and the lines. I'll trip through the whole play just doing sample speeches. Then I find, once I'm in my dressing room, the process of making-up particularly relaxing, because for me it's painting.

So, for whatever it takes, half an hour to an hour, I have a very good relaxing time. And then, in the last half hour before the performance, once I'm now in costume and everything, I'll pace around and again will just do a few lines here and there.

SP: **I notice in the diaries that there seems to be something very self-critical about you?**

AS: Yes, there is.

SP: **Even still?**

AS: Yes, it's in my nature. I suppose I'm not a natural actor. And I think that's why the stage fright hit me as it did, of saying, 'You, Antony Sher, what are you doing?' Because I'm really still a shy little kid. I've never really outgrown that. In my teenage years, acting was liberating because I was allowed not to be that frightened little schoolboy.

But the main thing I've learnt about acting if I had to put it in one sentence is that it's got to be about you. It's not about disguise. It's about revealing yourself. It's about your visible soul, to borrow a phrase from Cyrano de Bergerac. The visible soul. I think that's the acting that moves me most when I see it. Judi Dench would be a perfect example. There's nothing better than that acting.

SP: **So, are there individual performances where you'll leave the stage and think, 'Yes, I got it tonight'? Or, are you always walking back to the dressing room and thinking, 'It was okay, but that scene wasn't great,**

and this scene wasn't great'? I'm just interested to know whether this self-critic is it still there, or are you kinder to yourself now?

AS: I think there are performances when we say to one another, 'It flew tonight.' Either the whole thing or individually. It's a wonderful feeling, and terribly frustrating because you've no idea why. And you certainly can't reproduce it at will. But it just happens that the whole thing flies. It's that perfect mixture of relaxation and concentration that makes for a great performance.

I always think that opera singers or ballet dancers, they have to be so much more skilled than we do as actors because they have to train their bodies to do specific things. And so, they're carrying an enormous amount of technique. But then, they fly when it's there, the technique is there, but their souls fly out. And just occasionally, you feel that as an actor.

14
Avoid Pointless Comparisons

When Sir Antony Sher got his big break at the RSC in 1984, some would say he had been handed the ultimate Shakespearean poisoned chalice. The part he was to play was the lead in *Richard III* – a part that had been so utterly colonised on stage and in film thirty years earlier by Laurence Olivier that any subsequent interpretation of the role was doomed to failure by comparison. Such was the reach of Olivier's Richard that, uniquely for a Shakespearean performance, it made its way into popular culture. The hunchback, the enormous nose, and the hissing, malevolent voice were all instantly recognisable – Peter Sellers even impersonated Olivier's Richard singing the Beatles' song 'A Hard Day's Night'!

What was a young actor, making his way in the business and caught in Olivier's dazzling spotlight, to do? As Sher told me, 'I thought it was impossible. [Olivier] had done it definitively.' But then he 'forced [himself] to think differently and found another way of playing it'. And how. Such was the success of Sher's Richard III, memorably lurching around the stage on crutches, that all subsequent portrayals were measured against *his*, and the whole cycle started over again.

I meet, and coach, many people in professional life who are crippled by the curse of comparison. Most large professional firms are stuffed full of extremely talented, intelligent people. And a certain kind of mind can be cowed by this sort of company and allow wholly unhelpful thought patterns to take root: 'I'm not as smart as X' or 'Y is a much better fit' or 'Z always gets the good work; she's more popular around here than me.'

It seems to me that this sort of mindset could do with considering the well-known psychological phenomenon 'survivorship bias'. This is the brain's tendency to focus on, well, survivors rather than 'non-survivors' when looking for evidence of how to operate. The most famous example of this process in action comes from the Second World War. The US military were trying to establish how to better protect their aircraft, which were tumbling from the skies in alarming numbers in the middle of their involvement in the war. The approach they adopted was to carefully examine the planes that returned, establish where they seemed to have incurred most damage (on the wings and tail), and fit extra protection to those specific areas. Unfortunately, there was absolutely no discernible improvement in the number of aircraft lost – until the issue was put before a team of mathematicians led by Abraham Wald. Wald immediately saw the flaw in the process: the military had been taking account only of the aircraft which returned. By definition, these aircraft could sustain attacks in the areas with the greatest number of gunshots, as they had returned safely to base. The parts of the planes which needed reinforcement were areas without visible damage – the engines, as it turned out – and the evidence of this could only be garnered from fallen planes, not returning ones. Wald's observation was put into practice with success, and it demonstrates the value of standing back from a situation and ensuring our frame of reference is the most accurate one.

When we compare ourselves unfavourably to our peers, or to the tiny cadre of people who rise to the top of any profession, we are lacking the appropriate frame of reference. What about the many hundreds of applicants who failed to be selected for a training contract? Or the thousands who, for whatever reason, didn't gain the requisite grades to even be considered for a job like ours?

When we consider our achievements in this wider context, chances are we have done pretty well, and that the relentless pressure we feel to be better than X or Y is unnecessary. But a further 'mind warp' sometimes takes place when we consider our peers: we over-estimate their competence and underestimate their luck. Often, senior players in an industry got where they are because they happened to be in the right place at the right time. There was nothing objectively superior about them – it was simply a matter of timing.

Before we bemoan our own lack of luck, it may be worth considering the work of Richard Wiseman, a psychology professor at the University of Hertfordshire, who has researched the subject of luck in some detail – even to the point of running a Luck School to teach unlucky people how to act more like lucky ones!

'What the work shows as a whole,' he writes in his excellent book *The Luck Factor*, 'is that people can change their luck. Luck is not something paranormal in nature. It's something that we are creating by our thoughts and behaviour.'[18] He goes on to point out that 'lucky' people are more in the habit of maximising opportunities – saying yes to whatever life throws their way – than 'unlucky' ones, who tend to play all the angles in their head before committing, by which time the opportunity may well have passed.

---

18   R Wiseman, *The Luck Factor: The scientific study of the lucky mind* (Arrow, 2004)

So, beware the debilitating practice of comparing yourself to others and feeling that you come up short. There are inevitably many more people who are *less* successful than us – we just don't tend to acknowledge them. And those who may be more successful than us could have 'luck' to thank – or their willingness to seize opportunities that we might pass over.

In the end, like Sir Antony Sher, we need to avoid comparing ourselves with others, no matter how long the shadow they cast over us, and get on with creating our own performance.

KEY QUESTIONS

1. Are you comparing yourself to the full field or to the outliers?

2. Do we learn more from those who do (success) or those who don't (failure)?

3. How often do you make your own luck by taking advantage of the opportunities that come your way?

15
Manage Your Inner Critic

'You are a f****** idiot. Why did you even think that? Completely crazy idea – you will make yourself look foolish if you say that out loud.'

'Why don't you ever learn? You're no good at things like this. You are a fraud, and it can only be a matter of time before everyone else realises it.'

'Nobody likes you. Nobody rates you. Face it, in this type of setting you're just not up to the mark. Leave it to the confident types to do all the talking and just merge into the background somehow, you a**hole.'

Yep, just some brief excerpts from the conversation I have with myself several times a day. It's a never-ending drone, spreading misery and sapping energy all the time. The weird thing is, until a particularly useful spell of therapy, I didn't even know it was there. It was just the soundtrack to my life – self-generated muzak that seemed normal and natural and, well, deserved.

'You are very harsh on yourself,' the therapist said.

'I'm not harsh on myself,' I replied. 'I just wish I'd achieved more professionally, wasn't such a ****head in social situations and hadn't made such a complete and utter ****up of my personal life.'

There was silence as the therapist let my words sink in.

'Oh,' I said. 'I see what you mean.'

From that moment on, I started to be aware of my inner critic. His verbal diarrhoea. His unvarying tone of rage and indignation. And I used a technique the therapist had recommended: write down these words, and imagine how I would feel if they were directed at my friends, or my children. Needless to say, I was appalled. I spoke to myself in a way that would not be in any way acceptable to speak to someone else.

I know I'm not alone. Many of the top professionals I work with suffer from this. Call it 'imposter syndrome', call it 'perfectionism', it's all the same thing: a tendency to self-sabotage. A little voice in your head that tries to undermine you at every stage – the ultimate unreliable narrator who is unfortunately chronicling the story of your life.

One of the most moving stories I heard when researching the book was Sir Antony Sher's battle with stage fright. Already a distinguished, experienced actor, with decades of experience behind him, he suddenly had to deal with a voice in his head that was hell-bent, night after night, on interrupting his concentration, infecting his performance and diluting his power. For any of us, the inner critic is a nuisance. For an actor onstage, the problem is existential. It could have been the end of Sher's career. Instead, he faced it down, accepted a one-man show and 'kill or cure', neutered the critic and rediscovered the actor's voice.

If we are to thrive, we need to optimise our resources. And one of our most important resources is what we tell ourselves about ourselves. Once we notice that inner voice, and realise that its tone is overtly critical and non-constructive, action must be taken. But what action?

The answer lies in retraining the critic to be compassionate. Most of us presumably feel the most appropriate way to engage with someone who is suffering is with compassion rather than criticism, and we need to adopt the same approach with ourselves. For high-performing professionals, this is often extremely hard to do.

To get a better understanding of how to face down the inner critic, I spoke with Dr Chris Irons. He is one of the founding board members of the Compassionate Mind

Foundation, a charitable organisation that aims to promote wellbeing through the scientific understanding and application of compassion.

'It's important to notice the self-critic when it arises – like a cut finger, it's hard to do something helpful about this inner voice if you don't notice when it's activated,' he advises.

'When you notice it, it's useful to try to "be" with this inner voice in a different way – rather than just going along with what it says, or trying to fight it off or ignore it. Becoming familiar with what it is saying and why it might be saying it at that moment can give you more information about it.

Generally, it can be useful to learn why it might be doing what it's doing. For example, if you imagined for a moment that it was possible to never experience self-criticism again – are there any concerns or fears that emerge if you imagine living your life without the critic being there (for example: being lazy, making mistakes, getting angry at others, becoming 'too big for your boots')?

Once we understand how our self-critic is often trying to protect us from other fears, it can then be useful to start bringing a more caring and compassionate response to it; so, it might be possible to recognise that although unpleasant, self-criticism is often about protecting us in some way.

Try to shift from self-criticism to compassionate self-correction so that, when we notice that critical voice in our heads, we shift to a more supportive, caring response instead. If a friend were being critical with themselves for something similar, how would you try to support them? What would you say? What would you want for them?'

For many professionals, this may sound a bit soft. But for Chris Irons, the compassionate version of yourself is 'wise, caring and strong'. It is the embodiment of the airline mantra to fasten your own oxygen mask before helping others. If the voice in your own head is not caring and compassionate, you are making your chance of surviving and thriving so much more difficult.

KEY QUESTIONS

1. How often do you notice your own inner critic?
2. What is it protecting you from?
3. What might a more compassionate approach to yourself sound like?

16

Identify A 'Self-soothing' Ritual

When Sir Antony Sher was describing what it is like to prepare to step out on stage in front of 1,000 people, he mentioned a phrase that David Tennant had taught him: 'panic management'. Many actors are superstitious and will develop elaborate and unvarying rituals ahead of their calls to the stage. Sher's involves arriving early, warming up alone and 'tripping through' most of his speeches in his head. It is a way of imposing order on terror: of morphing the anxiety of an opening night, say, or a new venue, into the familiarity of any other performance.

Likewise, in sport, players will often follow similar rituals. These can involve 'trigger' words or processes.

When Rory McIlroy won the Open Championship in 2014, he revealed afterwards (in an interview with ESPN) that, 'I've got a couple of trigger words I've been using this week, that I keep telling myself in my head just as I'm about to hit [the ball].'

The point is that professional actors and sportspeople have to find a way to deal with the fear and panic that their high-stress occupations present to them every day. If they could not overcome the mental chatter and fear of failure that accompanies these sorts of moments, they simply wouldn't be able to do their jobs. No actor makes their name in the wings, and no golfer lifts a trophy by being unable to hit the ball off the tee.

What I think is interesting about these examples is that the individuals have planned for their 'brain freeze' moment. They know it will happen. And they put in place a ritual, mental or physical, that helps provide a mixture of comfort, familiarity and focus.

In professional life, giving presentations is often the source of the kind of anxiety that has the power to freeze the brain and turn otherwise competent individuals to jelly. In the course of my career I have worked with dozens and dozens of people preparing for keynote presentations, and the principal question I get asked by them is always the same: 'How do I control my nerves?' There is no magic formula, but what I will try and do is help them develop a ritual of their own for the moments immediately before they start their presentation, when nerves can often threaten to render them speechless. I try and get them concentrating on two or three simple tasks that can almost happen on auto-pilot – tasks that get them into their introduction almost before they know what is happening.

First, I have them counting the breaths as they wait to get to their feet. Breathe in through the nose, out through the mouth, count one on the exhale, just get to twenty…

Then, there is a ritual for when they reach the podium: Notes placed on the lectern. A sip of water, raising the glass with their right hand. A side-step to their left away from the podium before they begin…

Then comes their first line. I am not a fan of scripted presentations, but I always suggest the first few lines are scripted and memorised. The presenters want to be so grooved in those opening lines that they trip off the tongue with no effort whatsoever – they don't have to be actively sought for or memorised.

By now, the heart rate should have moderated, the feeling of nausea will have passed, and the presenter can get on with the business of engaging with the audience. But without that little three-stage ritual, practised endlessly in advance, I know that some people I have worked with would not have been able to get to their feet at all.

You will have your own nightmare scenarios – the kind of things that keep you awake at night in fearful anticipation or cause you to freeze if they happen to you without warning. The key is to find a ritual – like a word you repeat to yourself or a physical action – that you can rely on to get you out of freeze-or-flight mode and that allows you to function and to execute your professional skillset.

Practising mindfulness is one of the principal ways we can get some control over frantic and counterproductive thought patterns. In the last ten years, mindfulness has evolved from something many professionals would view with some cynicism as airy-fairy mystic nonsense. It is mainstream now, its value unquestioned, and several friends of mine, once high-flying partners at global firms, have left their lofty corporate perches to become mindfulness teachers!

One of my favourite mindfulness quotes, and an encapsulation of why a mindfulness ritual may be helpful when anticipating a work event that threatens your professional equilibrium, comes from Theravadan Buddhist monk Bhante Gunaratana:

> 'Mindfulness gives you time. Time gives you choices. Choices, skilfully made, lead to freedom. You don't have to be swept away by your feeling. You can respond with wisdom and kindness rather than habit and reactivity.'[19]

---

19 Bhante Gunaratana, *Beyond Mindfulness in Plain English* (Wisdom Publications, 2009)

KEY QUESTIONS

1. What are the situations in your professional life which tend to make you panic?

2. What practice have you identified to help you 'self-soothe'?

3. What mindfulness training does your organisation offer?

17
Eat Smart

One of the interesting aspects of working with clients in different parts of the world is being able to compare and contrast different cultural approaches to food and work. This is particularly evident at lunchtime, where approaches vary from a two-hour communal activity involving the whole team going off-site for several courses to the snatched sandwich at the desk wiping crumbs from the keyboard.

Any discussion of how to optimise yourself for peak performance in a professional role cannot possibly avoid talking about diet and nutrition. It's a subject where we all know the basics but often find the application of them difficult. I decided to consult an expert in the field, Rosie Letts. Rosie is a qualified and registered nutritional therapist with many years' experience of helping busy people fit an appropriate diet into demanding lives.

I wondered if there were some basic questions people needed to ask themselves in order to assess the efficacy of their current diets. Rosie came up with three:

'The first thing I always say is, "How do you feel when you wake up in the morning?" So if you're waking up feeling groggy, if you're tired, if getting up is a struggle, if you're immediately stressed, checking your phone etc., things aren't right.

So you should be able to naturally wake up, ideally before your alarm, and feel at peace, feel pain-free, feel without inflammation, without headache, and generally feel motivated for the day ahead. So that's the first thing: the way that you feel when you wake up in the morning.

The second thing I'd look for is: is my energy, is my focus, is my enthusiasm constant throughout the day? So also ask whether there's any kind of pattern to your energy, whether you get any slumps, whether you know that the morning's the best time for you and by the afternoon you're a little bit hopeless, so you're not scheduling meetings then.

Because really, if your nutrition's good, if your diet's working for you, you shouldn't be experiencing these big fluctuations in energy. And if you are experiencing big slumps after food or in the afternoon, more than likely that's to do with your diet, and potentially you've got food intolerance, you've got a problem with your digestion that's making you feel very sluggish after food.

Or potentially it's whatever you're eating, you're going for carbohydrate-rich foods or you're grabbing a sandwich, and that's not fuelling the right neurotransmitter production in your brain, so it's making you tired and sleepy rather than making you feel alert and energised. So there are simple changes, we can restructure diets in order to account for that.

And then, the third thing I would say is, "Do I want to do exercise, do I feel like I've got energy, is that appealing? And does the exercise make me feel revitalised, as it should, or does it make me feel drained?"

So as work-lives tend to get busier and busier, and particularly if you're flying between different time zones, exercise is usually one of the first things to go, and people always say it's because "I haven't got time"; it's not because they haven't got time, it's almost always because they're out of kilter, they're not feeling well in themselves, so exercise stops being appealing.

And then, sometimes when people do train, because their nutrient stores are depleted, when people are very, very stressed, they run through B vitamins at a really alarming rate, and so actually doing workouts is exhausting rather than refreshing and revitalising, as it should be.'

Having run the diagnostic, I wondered if there were some quick wins that busy professionals could put in place if they felt their energy levels could do with improving? Or is it the case that we need a complete life overhaul? Rosie offers the following advice:

'So, all I would say is for a few days just try having a high-protein and high-vegetable lunch. Try having fish and salad. Depends what's available in canteens, but most people have got access to places like Pret, and you can choose an option which is a stodgy carbohydrate or go for protein and vegetables and just observe how you feel in the afternoon.

In terms of the three practical steps that most people can easily do which will make the biggest difference, eating breakfast is absolutely crucial. If you eat within two hours of waking up and you make sure that what you're eating has got a high protein element, and ideally some fruit or vegetables as well, you set your blood sugar levels for the day.

The second thing I'd say is hydration is as important as nutrition. And again, it's one of the things that everyone knows but a lot of people don't do anything about. Poor hydration really affects your focus, your concentration, but it can also really, really affect your mood.

So just a simple process of carrying a water bottle with you wherever you go, making sure the first thing you do in the morning is have a glass of water, making sure every time you eat you have a glass of water. If people are really struggling, there are apps that they can use. There's one called Drink Water. And literally, you programme in how much water you want to drink, and every hour it sets an alarm and tells you to drink a glass of water. It's that simple, but it works because actually it's not a difficult thing to do; it's just getting into that habit.

And the third thing I'd say is just really simply eat more vegetables. People don't eat anything like enough vegetables. And if you start eating more vegetables, literally in any form, it will start to fuel the beneficial bacteria in your gut and it will bring down inflammation in your body. And it's a really good way to get all the vitamins you need as well. Just think about: "Is there colour on my plate? Am I eating beige food, or can I inject some colour into this?"

In this day and age, you can eat incredibly well on the run, it's just a case of checking yourself, checking what you're doing. Are you buying a cheese baguette or have you considered the other options, salads and soups, other things that are available? Pretty much, even at airports, there are better options available.'

And so, if you are interested in de-beigeing your diet, I'd suggest you head to Rosie Letts' website, www.rosielettsnutrition.com

---

KEY QUESTIONS

1. How refreshed do you feel when you wake up in the morning?
2. Is your energy level consistent throughout the day?
3. Do you feel motivated to exercise?

18
Help Other People – Gain Perspective

Simon is a partner at a large international firm, and he heads a practice that could legitimately be called market-leading. He spends much of his time in the air, as his client base is largely situated across Asia. He is often quoted in the press and makes occasional forays onto Bloomberg television. He appears to embody a talented professional at the height of his powers. And yet, a couple of years ago, he came close to burnout.

'It's interesting looking back on it,' he tells me. 'It wasn't a sudden volcanic event that left me stretched out on the canvas. It wasn't dramatic at all. It was more a sort of slow, creeping lethargy. The sort of feeling you get on Sunday nights of "oh, I wish the weekend was a bit longer" but which then takes over your mind most of the time, and you're literally dragging yourself to meetings. A sense of "I don't want to be here", which of course you're having to fight all the time because you can't let that show to clients and colleagues.'

He sought professional help and realised this wasn't just a blip but a long-running depression which he had been ignoring for some time.

> 'Fortunately, my firm was very understanding. I did take time away, I did find a very effective therapist and I did start to get much more aware of what it takes to keep your mental health on an even keel. In my kind of job you can just keep turning a blind eye to the symptoms because if you're on that kind of treadmill, you can't stop running or you think you'll fall flat on your face.'

On his return to work, Simon made several changes to his approach. There was more time set aside for exercise and less time in the air. He followed a dietary plan. And, most surprising of all to him, he got involved in the firm's pro bono programme.

> 'My team all laugh at this because they know how little time I had for this before I took time out. The firm is involved in many charitable initiatives, and indeed there is an expectation that you will spend a certain amount of your

time every year doing this stuff. I always dismissed it in the past. We're here to make money, not be do-gooders. But my time around the corner has been a revelation.'

By 'around the corner' he means an inner-city London high school, where, every week since his return to work, Simon has been helping with the reading programme. He spends an hour of his time helping some of the country's least advantaged children to read. The benefits of participating in the programme have been unexpected.

'It's absolutely not me feeling smug and self-satisfied that I have given some of my precious time to these kids. Or that I scuttle back to our plush office feeling, "Thank God I work here and not there." I have found the work to be genuinely inspiring. The staff at the school, the sense of mission they have about their work, really impress me. And the way they, and the kids, have challenged me. One of the kids forgot his reading book one day and I was quite sharp and said, "You need to sort yourself out. You wouldn't get away with that sort of approach where I work." And this kid just eyeballed me with complete disdain, and afterwards one of the teachers pulled me aside and said, "You won't get anywhere with that kind of tone. You need to find a different approach." And she was right. I can be contemptuous of people, and in my daily work that would never ever be challenged. But it *was* challenged at the school, and I have worked really hard to find a way of supporting these kids that works for them. And when you feel like you have made a connection, and when there is a bit of a light going on in them when they feel they have achieved, it's a great feeling.'

One of the limitations of a career in any of the professional services is that you can end up working in a sealed environment, cut off from the rest of the world. That's why getting involved in some charitable work, like Simon demonstrates, can be so therapeutic. It takes us out of our familiar environment, helps us put our own travails in some sort of perspective, and can enable us to discover new capabilities within ourselves.

There are many ways of helping others. Internally, it may involve mentoring someone at the start of their career. Externally, it can be about using your professional skills to help an organisation that would otherwise never be able to afford them. Some people get so absorbed with a particular cause that they may act as trustees or even set up their own charities. Many professionals have found this kind of work helpful because it seems imbued with a meaning their day jobs sometimes lack. For one individual, it was seeing a quote pinned up on a training room wall that resonated:

'The purpose of life is not to be happy. It is to be useful, to be honourable, to be compassionate, to have it make some difference that you have lived and lived well.'

'I didn't think much of the training course, but the message really resonated,' they said. 'I think you are blessed if you can make a difference in your day job. But if it's not that kind of world, then you can diversify. You can find volunteering opportunities that speak to that need. And I went out and got involved in our not-for-profit initiatives that have really given me some balance and sense of making a difference in my life.'

KEY QUESTIONS

1. What charitable opportunities are open to you?

2. How much time do you spend in an environment quite different to the one you work in?

3. Do you feel you are 'making some difference' to other peoples' lives?

19
The Telecoms Entrepreneur: Shirin Dehghan

Many people think they have a game-changing business idea. But the number who actually manage to bring their ideas to fruition, let alone sell them for millions, is incredibly low. Shirin Dehghan not only did this; she did it as a female engineer of Iranian origin. The start-up world is not known for its commitment to diversity; the number of female entrepreneurs securing start-up finance is still pitifully low, so to say that Shirin overcame extraordinary odds is an understatement. But the facts don't lie: she built a ground-breaking telecoms business, Arieso, and sold it in 2013 for a cool $85 million USD.

SP: So, reading about your story, there are setbacks along the way that you would find in many entrepreneurial journeys: the difficulty with having funding withdrawn at one stage, and a key contract being lost, and those kinds of things. I'm just really interested, what is it that persuaded you that, actually, these setbacks weren't fatal?

SD: Obviously each of those could have been fatal in a start-up. Any kind of withdrawal of funding or anything like that, cash is the most important thing that you can have in a start-up. If you don't have it, it's game over. So I think the thing that drove me forward was the sheer thinking that this is going to work. I looked at problems as obstacles to get over. And I think that really positive outlook was what drove me forward.

SP: Is that the engineer in you? Looking at a problem as something to be solved.

SD: Well, exactly. So giving up wasn't really part of my vocabulary ever. And I think that mindset of the training that you get as an engineer: you have a problem, and you come up with a solution, and that's how it works. And you keep going until you solve it. And I think that's sort of what's really kept me going.

SP: What about the tolerance for risk, though? Because it seems to me you put quite a lot on the line at several points in your journey.

SD: I think for any entrepreneur you have to be by nature someone who is not afraid of doing something that you've never done before. You're not going to be fazed by situations you've never come across before. And that's a personal journey. When you start you don't know everything, obviously.

And so, in my space, I was a very good engineer, but I had no idea about the commercial side. I had to learn all that. But that's okay for me. So, if I don't know it, I can learn. It's that confidence that I think pushed me forward. And I think once you have that confidence of the unknown, that you can handle the unknown, you'll never be fazed by anything.

SP: There's also something that came through in a talk I was watching that you gave at Southampton University, which was about putting a team together. And I wonder whether your ability to carry on through that journey is about also recognising your own limitations and where you need to bring in help? You seem to have assembled a great team very early on.

SD: Yes, that's one key lesson from my journey – I always knew what I was good at, and I also knew what I was not good at. And certain things took me a while to realise, that I wasn't good at them, and it was better to bring some people on board to do this job. But I think that the realisation of being able to be self-aware, and also just assemble the base team.

My biggest asset was the ability to attract really top people into the company. And I wasn't afraid to do it. I went out of my way to hire this amazing technical person out of their lab. He was based in the US; I was a small company in the UK. And I never was fazed by, 'Oh my God, this guy works for the biggest, the best technical company in the world, in my sector, and there's no way he's going to…' I never had that mindset.

I just felt that I need that person because of his background and his knowledge, and I'm going to get it. So very early on in my journey I managed to hire a former CTO of Vodafone. So at that stage I was an engineer with just ten years of technical track record, and the business track record, but I still had the ability to just pick up the phone and get this guy.

This ability was something that I'd never realised I had. But sometimes there are things about yourself that you don't know that you have.

I was very good at persuading people – not just to join my company, but to actually buy my product. I was very good at selling. And those qualities I never knew I had, but I also knew that I needed the best people as a team, to come on board professionally. So I think that combination of being able to hustle and get the best people on board, and realising what I wasn't good at, was one of the key elements of the success for me.

SP: And pretty non-compromising as well, even if that meant upsetting your husband.[20]

SD: Oh, yes. I'm still married to him! Yes, everybody gets really shocked that I say that, but at the end of the day, the way I thought about it was that this is my business, and I needed to make a success of it, and if that meant I had to make difficult decisions, I had to do that. It wouldn't have mattered. If it was my mother, I would have done exactly the same thing. It's not being disrespectful to the other person. To me, if a change

---

20 Shirin asked her husband to step down from his position as CTO in the company

was needed, it just needed to be made, and no matter who that person would be, or was…

And I think that's something that a lot of, now that I've worked with lots of different founders, actually they have real difficulty with, making those tough decisions and tough choices. But they founded a company with a mate from university, and they go back a long way, they don't want to upset them and things like that. Yes, I was lucky that I never fell into that category.

I just needed to get the job done, I needed a team that would get the job done, and I was… It's a bit of a mercenary way of looking at it, but it wasn't for me, it was for the company, and everyone else was really happy about it. So everyone knew what I was doing.

People understood that if you didn't perform, then that's it. They're not going to last a long time in that company.

SP: **You are a tech entrepreneur. So to what extent is technology the answer, or only partly the answer? The reason I ask: we're in an age where a lot of people think immediately that technology is the answer to everything. Where do you stand on that?**

SD: I think technology obviously can help, but it's not the answer… I don't think it's the answer to everything. I think that people underestimate the power of people on their own. So I know there's a lot of talk about AI and it's going to revolutionise the future, but then again, you look at the environment, and you're thinking to yourself, well, technology's not going to solve that. It's our individual behaviours that are going to ultimately make an impact, or not make an impact.

So I think on that basis, technology can definitely help make a massive impact. But I think it's being responsible with it.

SP: **And how attached are you to your mobile phone?**

SD: Oh, very attached. Sometimes I think to myself, 'Oh my God, I'm a part of the industry that created this monster.' And it's an addiction, it's terrible. I'm a lot better now, and now I do have a couple of hours when I don't think about it, which wasn't at all the case before. But yes, it's not good. But again, it comes back to technology and how do we use it responsibly.

SP: **Do you think we're only just beginning to understand that? How we use it responsibly?**

SD: Yes. I think so. I think we're in an age where technology is way ahead. But now we're seeing the consequences of its impact. And I think that's making people realise that we need to take a step back and look at how we use technology. Because technology, I think, is not bad. It's wonderful to have AI diagnose breast cancer far more accurately than a radiologist or a doctor.

So I think all of that is excellent. But I do think that as human society we just need to be aware of how technology is impacting not just our lives but our planet, the things we all care about.

SP: **You grew up in Iran.**

SD: Yes.

SP: **I don't know how many young women in Iran thought of an engineering career and thought of themselves**

as a highly successful entrepreneur. Can you tell me? How unusual was that, and if it was unusual, what was it about you that dared to be different?

SD: I often wonder what my life would have been like if my parents didn't decide to emigrate to the UK back in 1984. This was after the revolution and three years into the Iran/Iraq war. And the answer's very simple. I am obviously formed as the person who I am by that stage: the encouragement, the drive and all the important other stuff. So that wouldn't have changed.

But there's no way I would have had the same opportunities in Iran as I did in the UK. It is a fact of life that in Iran women do not get the same opportunities as men. And that has a big impact, obviously, on their progress. And that doesn't mean that they don't progress. And in fact, I was very surprised when, with my company, this is a long time ago, probably fifteen, sixteen years ago, that I actually went to Iran to try [to] sell my product to one of the telecom companies there.

And I was asked to give a talk to the engineers that worked in the design area of the mobile telecoms company in Iran. I was happy to give a talk, expecting to go into a room full of men. And actually, when I went into the room, half of the room was women. There were women there, 50%. And I was taken aback by this image of literally half the room being women engineers.

First of all, I was really proud because I felt, wow, you guys are definitely beating the UK at this. And second was that I actually felt that things were obviously changing for the better, since the time that I'd left Iran. So there were two levels of encouragement. But as we moved up the level in the organisation, obviously women weren't present in the top management.

So I think that the answer to your question is, I think that as a result of the restrictions that had been placed on women in Iran, it has made them even more determined than before. And they may have more than 50% at university.

But certainly, they do not have available opportunities that I had. The reason I succeeded was because I came from a background where I knew what it was like not to have those opportunities, and when I was presented with the opportunities in this country I took them with both hands. And I think that also some of my success is because of my background, because I knew what it was like to be treated as a second-class citizen, and not being given the same level of worth, shall we say.

And when you are given that opportunity, that equal opportunity in a different environment, you know how to look after it and how to make the most of it. That's probably one of the reasons. I do realise that I'm one of the rare women, as an engineer, and Iranian, there aren't many people like me. And that have an amazingly successful business, as well. I do realise that. And I think my background very much contributed to me doing what I did.

SP: **Okay. Final question. So this is more looking at the work you do now. When you're looking at entrepreneurs to invest in, aside from the validity of** the idea, what kind of attributes are you looking for, given what you know about the journey they're likely to have to undertake?

SD: I look at three criteria. The most important things: Team. Market. Product. And the team is, I think, really critical. And the thing that I look for is the ability to adapt. Because in business you just don't know what might get thrown at you. You may have to go through a recession; are you strong enough to make people redundant and save cash?

Is this person capable of attracting top-quality talent into his or her company? That ability, I think, is one of the critical factors. Because in a really competitive environment, in a start-up, without a business track record to speak of, to attract the best players, to project the right level of charisma and vision and just get those people, gives a clear competitive edge.

20
Nurture The Tribe

For all the positivity which characterises many of the points in this book, I have become more and more aware that positivity alone is not enough to be optimised in a professional setting; there needs to be a counterbalance. And that doesn't mean pessimism or cynicism – although God knows both of these are present in abundance in professional life. The counterbalance is realism; in particular, realism about one's own limitations. Shirin Dehghan provides a great example of this. She came up with the idea for her business, and she got it off the ground. But very early on, she realised her own lack of commercial experience would be a problem as the business grew, and she went about assembling a team of complementary talents who would be able to compensate for her areas of weakness.

Being optimised in professional life means understanding your limitations as an individual practitioner and realising the greater value you can deliver as part of a team.

This requires a certain humility that doesn't come easily to everyone. A law firm partner told me:

> 'You do still get some people who like to operate as lone wolves, who are secretive about what they are doing and reluctant to share information and clients. But I think they are far less prevalent than they would have been ten, fifteen years ago. As the work has become more specialised, and the deals more complex, that approach just isn't viable. You need people who can contribute effectively to a team effort, and realise that by doing so they are leveraging their own expertise in a way that would be impossible if they operated alone.'

So, at a senior or founder level, the key skill is the ability to spot gaps in your own skillset or wider offering and hire aggressively to fill those gaps – not to mention (often the most difficult part) keeping the whole team in alignment once recruitment is complete.

At a more junior level, optimisation means finding a niche and filling it effectively – balancing the need to demonstrate one's own skillset with the requirement to support and facilitate colleagues to do the same.

Given that most professionals work as part of a team, it is surprising that the nature of effective teamwork is not better explored in many firms. In fact, to fully understand the essential dynamics of teams, you would need to turn to the military, not business. Teamwork in military environments is, of course, not desirable but essential, and the way the military prepares its recruits to operate effectively in a team leaves nothing to chance. The US military, in particular, has made a sizeable contribution to research on team dynamics, and many of its findings are in the public domain. The US Army's latest guidelines on team building should be essential reading for any practice leader anywhere in the world.[21]

The guidelines make it clear that for a team to function effectively, trust and good communication are key. Trust can be developed through a range of means, such as by positive affirmation – telling colleagues that their work is of high standard, that their judgement can be relied upon – and making effective use of breaks – because they provide 'opportunities for team members to talk about the issues they address in an informal, non-threatening way'. The way new members are welcomed into the team is critical: 'Teams [should] consider a version of a personal storytelling activity that provides new team members an opportunity to

---

21 Headquarters, Department of the Army (2015) *Army Team Building*, US Army Techniques Publication 6-22.6. https://armypubs.army.mil /epubs/DR_pubs/DR_a/pdf/web/atp6_22x6%20FINAL.pdf

tell the team a little about themselves.' (This in an army manual!)

Likewise, best practice in communication within a team is there in black and white. Acknowledging differences, understanding non-verbal communication, clarifying, active listening, and acknowledging communication with immediate and unambiguous feedback are all codified and part of the training. These skills are as important in the office as on the battleground, but how many professionals consciously master them?

Away from the military context, the ability to facilitate dialogue within a team – and, in particular, to ensure that minority or dissenting voices have airtime – is a valuable skill. Indeed, the research suggests that this can make a major contribution to the effectiveness of a team and as such presents an opportunity to even the most junior member, as a mid-level auditor explained to me:

> 'One thing I realised quite early on, especially when dealing with cross-border or cross-functional teams, is that nobody listens. Everybody wants their view prioritised, everyone is better at the talking than the listening, especially on these conference calls where you get lots of parties just jabbering away. And you often get quite introverted people whose views never get heard. I really try and listen out for that. If there's a view that

is expressed quite quietly and is immediately drowned out by other people, but seems to me to have some merit, I will shout over everyone else and get that person involved in the conversation, almost seize airtime on their behalf. Because I am very extroverted and don't find it hard to get heard, but I also know there are plenty of smarter people than me who deserve a hearing. And there have been a handful of occasions when just getting other views heard, shutting down the usual suspects, has delivered a view that has changed the game.'

Team settings allow us to flourish. The whole is greater than the parts. In the best teams, as in the ones Ann Daniels leads across the frozen wastes, the welfare of each individual is of paramount importance, and the team is motivated to ensure each member achieves more as part of the collective than they could ever do alone. It follows, then, that an important part of survival in professional life is not only to find a tribe you fit into but to find a unique and committed way to contribute to its success.

KEY QUESTIONS

1. Are you part of a team where your own skillset is complemented?

2. How do you ensure new team members feel welcome?

3. What contribution do you make on an ongoing basis to your team?

21
Sort Out Sleep

When you discuss the importance of, say, diet and exercise with the average professional, they will furrow their brow, nod sagely and recount their latest escapade at the new gym or with a cookbook by the latest food guru. When you bring up the subject of sleep, however, the reaction tends to be different. There's a sigh and a shake of the head and a sense that this is one for the 'write off' category. They know sleep is important, but it's the nature of the job, the 'always on' culture. The old eight hours a night is a pipe dream, but maybe if they are lucky they can catch up on some shut-eye at the weekend.

Sleep and professional life, it seems, just don't mix.

From the point of view of optimisation, this approach is madness. For proof, look at the attention paid to sleeping patterns by elite sports teams. When British Cycling looked to put its sport in the national consciousness by winning Olympic medals and, ultimately, the Tour de France, one of Sir Dave Brailsford's targets for 'marginal gains' was the cyclists' approach to sleep. And the man he listened to on the subject was the UK's most prominent 'sleep coach', Nick Littlehales.

Nick's story is fascinating. Starting off as an executive at one of Europe's largest bed manufacturers, he began to enquire if the largest sports franchises in the country were interested in taking sleep more seriously to provide a possible competitive advantage. Among the first to reply was Sir Alex Ferguson, and Nick spent the 1990s giving sleep advice to the fabled class of '92 at Manchester United – Ryan Giggs, David Beckham, et al. He went on to work with other leading football clubs around the world, plus Olympians and Paralympians. His approach to rest and recovery is so valued by the big franchises because they buy into the link between rest and performance – and Nick helps optimise that rest period.

His approach, as I found out when I got the chance to speak with him, is radical – with plenty to teach the average professional who frets about getting enough sleep. For Nick, the key is to think of sleep in terms of 90-minute cycles per week, rather than hours per night.

The key aim is to get thirty-five cycles in a week (52.5 hours), *not all of which are nocturnal.*

'We need to think *poly*phasically, not *mono*phasically about sleep,' Nick told me.

> 'Before the lightbulb first entered our lives, the human being would never try and sleep in one block just at night. There would be a shorter sleep at night, and a recovery sleep in the middle of the day, what in some cultures still exists and is called a siesta. But we are a monophasic generation, and so we think we can only sleep in one block at night. Now in the recent past this was still possible – my father's generation worked 9 to 5, and at the weekend he came home and cut the grass. The one block of sleep was fine. The trouble is we've moved into an era where that one block is no longer possible. Mainly because of technology, that night-time period has been interrupted, truncated. But as a species, we still need the eight hours recovery. And if we think polyphasically, we can get still that time and be much more productive.'

Nick recommends that four of the 90-minute rest cycles happen between 12 midnight and 6am. But then there is a need for a 30-minute nap, either in the middle of the day or in the early evening:

'Naps have got a bad name – people think in terms of the elderly or "snoozers are losers". And people always say, "I haven't got time for a nap, Nick." But if they ran their meetings more effectively, or cut down on some of the pointless internet surfing, most people could find that time. And the point is, the body *requires* that recovery time. You can either set aside time over lunch and in the early evening, or the body will decide to take its recovery time in the middle of an important call, or at your daughter's school play in the evening, or in the fast lane of the M4 when you are driving home. None of those is a good look.'

As well as the early-evening nap, Nick feels that people should be mindful of getting 2- or 3-minute 'recovery breaks' every 90 minutes during the day if they are serious about optimising their performance.

'By just going and having a conversation with a colleague for a couple of minutes and standing right next to the window or in the doorway, you are exposing yourself to 2,000 lux and stimulating yourself with serotonin. If you stood a metre inside the window, you wouldn't get that hit. Even going and half filling your water bottle and then coming back to your desk creates a mini recovery period. You only half fill it, because you want to get up and refill it again an hour or so later. And if you combine the four nocturnal phases with a short nap during the day and plenty of these mini recovery periods, something amazing will happen. You will be more alert and productive during the day and throughout the evening, and you will sleep better at night. You've taken the pressure off that night-time block. There will be less awakening, less going to the toilet and less anxiety.'

I ended my conversation with the sleep coach by asking if a better bed might be the answer. The reply was unambiguous.

'Most of the products that get advertised are bullshit. You're designed to sleep outside, as a human being. Whenever you go camping, off to the hills and the mountains, it's very quick – you become more reliant on circadian rhythms. You have a wonderful time sleeping in a tent. What actually matters is to look at the correct sleeping position: you should sleep along the opposite side to your dominant side. And then apply the basics: we came into the world sleeping polyphasically, and we need to go back to something far more natural: recovery in shorter periods, more often.'

KEY QUESTIONS

1. How many hours sleep do you think you get in an average week?

2. Could your routine accommodate an early-evening nap?

3. What are your opportunities for 'mini recovery periods' during the day?

22
Assemble 'Team You' And Ask For Their Help

One of the more fascinating insights about thriving under pressure that I gained when writing this book came from Ann Daniels. It was on the difference between men and women on polar expeditions. Men, she said, sometimes found it more difficult to ask for help. Even to the point of concealing serious injury, and thereby impeding the progress of the whole team, it was more important for an individual to appear infallible than ask for help. This is the 'superhero' persona in action – and in pressurised situations, it is almost always a liability.

But what if, despite your best efforts, you cannot generate a solution on your own? Then surviving and thriving becomes all about reaching out and asking for help – anathema to the superhero.

This pre-supposes you have someone to reach out to. And just as it is better to dig your well before you are dry, I notice that top performers are assiduous about cultivating the kind of support network that will help them out long before they actually need it. This is not something that can be magicked out of thin air – these are relationships that can take years to cement.

Just as any large organisation will have a supervisory board to oversee its operations, you need to assemble your own board of advisers: Team You. This will be a diverse group of individuals whom you can rely on to give a range of supports – the role can rarely be filled by one 'mentor' alone. The precise composition of your team is up to you, but based on my interviews for the book the following roles are indispensable:

Cheerleader – Sir Antony Sher's answer to why he didn't simply pack his bags and return to South Africa after repeated rejection from London's top drama schools was simple: 'My mother!' His mother told him repeatedly that it was the *schools* who had got it all wrong, not him. We all need someone who fills this role, someone who believes in us more completely than we believe in ourselves. If you are fortunate, there will be multiple people within your family who can pick you up when you feel down. If not, it might be a teacher or friend. I stress that analytical objectivity is not important here – it is more that, when the chips are down, there is someone you can rely on to back you without reservation.

Technician – this is someone who is more experienced than you at your professional specialism. It is someone you feel comfortable asking what you suspect is a silly question and getting back a reasoned, informed, non-patronising response.

Straight-talker – someone who will tell you if you have f***ed up. In my experience, people in this category are exceedingly rare, and as such they must be cherished if found. It is so easy to exist in an echo chamber, where the only views you hear are closely aligned to your own. The problem increases exponentially the more senior you get; you end up fooling yourself that you are right most of the time, forgetting that you are the easiest person to fool.

Connector – someone whose network is broader and deeper than yours, and who is generous about making introductions.

Of course, all relationships are reciprocal, and you will need to ask yourself what you are offering the members of Team You in return for their guidance. But the huge advantage of assembling this board of personal advisers when you are young is that the opportunity to assist someone starting out is often reward enough for more senior players – the older you are, the more likely you will need to offer a quid pro quo.

Having assembled the team, use it.

A senior partner I interviewed for this book was reflecting on the most stressful moment in her career. The incident she chose wasn't related to a particularly demanding client or some internal politics once she entered the partnership. It was an episode from much earlier in her career:

> 'The hours were brutal. But the central difficulty was the lack of control. If you cannot see any element of controlling your own life, it is very tough. Even down to the level of tidying your sock drawer or making that hair appointment, there has to be a part of your life you can control. But I was a leaf tossed in the wind at that time. I was beyond exhausted. And it just doesn't work long term…you burn out, you hand in your resignation. So I asked for help, and asking for help is sometimes the first step in taking back control of your life.'

KEY QUESTIONS

1. How comfortable are you asking for help?

2. How robust – and diverse – is your support network?

3. How honest with yourself are you about the need to address problems when they occur?

23
Celebrate Individual And Collective Achievement

The training that the new recruits to the Royal Marines Commandos undertake is known to be the most rigorous military training in the world. Following many weeks of parade ground drills, physical training and fieldcraft preparation, the training culminates in the legendary '30 miler'. This is a 30-mile march across some of the most arduous terrain in England, in full fighting order – over 30 pounds of kit – and the march must be completed in under eight hours. It is often undertaken in the harshest of weather conditions.

I was curious to know what drives these recruits on, to overcome whatever physical and psychological obstacles the training puts in their way. I spoke to Paul

Mattin, a former major in the Royal Marines, who has subsequently built a career as an expedition leader to some of the world's most out-of-the-way places.

'It's about the green beret,' Paul told me. (The dark green beret is worn exclusively by the Royal Marines Commandos.) 'So, there's a badge involved, which is quite special. That brand, that club that the guys then are very much joining on the completion of that test. They then go to an organisation that lives and breathes its values, its commando ethos. And of course, that's quite overt. It's humble. It's stuck to. But in the same breath, you know that you've joined something that is very special. So, that shared belief, ethos, values – that's very much there.'

I noticed how assiduously the Marines cultivate their ethos. The values – excellence, integrity, self-discipline and humility – were talked about repeatedly from day one of the Marines' existence. The history of the regiment was instilled in new recruits by a visit to the Royal Marines museum in Portsmouth. The green beret was not only the sign of a gruelling test passed – it was the sign of admission to an exclusive club with a proud and storied heritage.

The beret, then, was a powerful motivating factor in getting recruits through the hardship of the training. But in the training process itself, recruits are carefully set up to succeed, not fail. Paul Mattin again:

'[New recruits] are coming with X amount in their glass, and it probably isn't enough actually to see them through. So, we would never dream of putting somebody through their commando tests in the first week or second week. They just wouldn't have that residual level, depth and pedigree of resilience. So, it's a steady build. So, you're building it. And you're giving them a taste one week. Next week, trying a bit more. Trying a bit more next week, and it's dark. That's different. And it's raining the following week. And so, actually you get these layers. With a young Royal Marine, they'll finish the end of their training, and they will have gone through so many different iterations, and exercises, and rehearsals, that they will have built up this great databank of stuff.

And they can draw on that. So, the point of putting a young Royal Marine, in my case seventeen years old when I joined, through a 30-mile extravaganza across Dartmoor, after three or four commando tests and a big exercise, is so that you've got something to draw on. It's not just to say you're tough enough. It's actually to give them this incredible reference that they can then just reach back into.'

Carefully calibrated development. Progressive resilience or 'muscle memory'. And above all the strong motivational pull of joining an exclusive institution based on shared values, shared heritage and shared hardship.

Sound like any professional firm you know?

No, me neither.

And yet, if the Marines are so successful at getting seventeen-year-old raw recruits to complete an arduous training process and subsequently put their lives on the line for Queen and country, surely there is plenty here for professional firms to ponder as they strive to retain top talent and create genuine engagement among staff?

I'll offer three quick talking points here for those of you who lead teams or contribute to career development discussions.

Firstly, resilience in the Marines is built up gradually. Success in overcoming one set of obstacles is banked, and it provides the momentum to overcome the next, higher ones. How often is a young professional's development managed in this way? Too often I see people either thrown in at the deep end with a sink-or-swim mentality, or left to graze unattended in the long grass of administrative tedium. Neither approach builds up the resourcefulness required to operate under severe pressure at the top level.

Next, firms often overlook the power of overcoming adversity as part of a collective – the concept of 'shared hardship'. Paul Mattin spoke about this in connection with work he was doing with a professional rugby side:

> 'They believe in each other and they're in it together, rather than there being a hierarchy or a power gradient in there. When you see young academy players who are as important as the old hand who's got thirty-five England caps, and he speaks to that academy player as if he was an equal…then you know you're in the right sphere, in the right space. So, sharing that hardship equally, and celebrating the success at the end of it. Recognising what we've done. That I think is a really important step in creating a mature and resilient team.'

Taking the time as a team to celebrate success, to appreciate the challenges successfully overcome, is key to enabling everyone to have the courage to climb the next mountain. In professional life, it is a stage often entirely absent as teams move imperceptibly from one deal to the next.

Finally, if partnership is the goal for most professional careers, how can that goal resonate with something other than dollar signs? Several friends of mine have commented that attaining partnership, the crowning glory of their careers, was in fact an anti-climax. 'There was no celebration. Just an uncomfortable feeling that people who until recently had admired me as a talented junior now had me in their sights as a rival,' one told me.

The green beret has almost mystical significance for a new Marine – they have become the latest keeper of the flame. How can the ultimate destination of a professional career acquire a similar lustre?

KEY QUESTIONS

1. When delegating work to junior staff, how conscious are you of exposing them to progressively higher levels of pressure?

2. How often do you take the time to celebrate success as a team?

3. How seriously does your firm take its history and heritage?

24
Have A Plan B

Most professionals start their career full of vim and vigour, eager for the challenge of each new meeting-stuffed day. A lucky few end their careers in much the same way. For the rest of us, energy and enthusiasm wane. The trick is to realise when the gas tank is less than half full, and to take action before the needle hits the red zone.

> 'It was when I got back to work after the August break one year that I knew things weren't right. I just didn't have the appetite for it anymore. I was aware of literally going through the motions.'

I suspect many of us have experienced what Adam, a corporate lawyer, is talking about in the quote above, particularly at the end of a good summer, perhaps away from work spending time in the sun with family and friends. It's lethargy, staleness and a sense that work doesn't do it for us anymore. The temptation is to ignore this creeping realisation and 'crack on' – we have commitments after all, and on the whole we have little to complain about, the money is good, the colleagues are fine...

It is important to be honest with ourselves about the level of engagement we feel for our work. Everyone feels differing levels of engagements at various times, but are you in a short-term blip or a death spiral? If it's the latter, there is an urgent need to take control of the situation before it is taken out of our hands.

'I had seen it before in older partners,' says Adam. 'It starts off with them not being quite as on it as they used to be. Then it infects their dealings with colleagues and ultimately clients. At the start of your career you sometimes have to fake it to make it. Later on, if you're faking it you're dangerously close to breaking it.'

When Paul Mattin talked about the challenges of leading a team into the wilderness on one of his extraordinary expeditions, he said that there is only one category of individual who is a genuine liability, and who is better off calling it quits: the person who in their heart of hearts doesn't want to be there. When you know you don't want to be where you are, it starts to have a demoralising effect on yourself and others around you. Optimised you are certainly not; rather, you become a fugitive, forever on the run and hoping that you do just enough to serve time and avoid the dreaded tap on the shoulder.

In my experience of coaching people who are at this point in their career, when we get around to exploring options, the phenomenon of learned helplessness sometimes comes into play. This theory, first expounded by American psychologist Martin Seligman in 1972, suggests that in a situation where negative events appear to come our way at random and without any chance of control, we can pretty soon give up on our ability to effect change.

In the workplace, this translates to a life of SOS: Same Old Shit. Same challenges, same people, same problematic commute, same financial demands... same, same, same, and we are powerless to do anything about it.

This is patently false and a dangerous, dispiriting mindset if we allow it to fester unchallenged. Change is nearly always possible; it just depends on whether this needs to be evolutionary or revolutionary.

Evolution involves seeing what incremental changes are possible within your current role or organisation. Perhaps a change of office, change of responsibility or change of clients might revive you. I have known technical wizards find a whole new lease of professional life by immersing themselves in their firm's mentoring programme or exploring a brand-new market. Others have been granted a sabbatical and have returned to their posts after six months refreshed and renewed.

But it may be that, in order to feel genuinely optimised again, you need more radical change. There are plenty of people who just fell into a professional career because it seemed the easiest well-paid option. While the money and ambition provide plenty of motivating power in the first few years of a career, they may not prove sufficient beyond that. If you have an itch to do something totally different, I'd urge you to scratch it.

Of course, while Winston Churchill and Steve Jobs provide inspiring templates, pivoting mid-career and ensuring your second act is better than your first is by no means easy. And this is where the 'side hustle' becomes so important, not just in the middle of a career but at the very beginning. We believe in diversification when considering our investment portfolios, but rarely in our careers. We put our eggs in one basket in our early twenties and sometimes regret it for the rest of our lives.

The side hustle is an activity we love; it does not necessarily represent the best source of revenue generation early on in life, but it's one that is well worth nurturing. Adam, the lawyer we encountered earlier, found salvation in exactly this approach.

'To be honest, I think I should have been an architect. Buildings and creativity have always been passions of mine. So, from quite early on, I have bought and renovated properties and acquired a decent level of knowledge around property development. When I got to the stage in my legal career where I thought, "This is it, I've had enough of the daily grind," I had property income already in place. But more than that, I was able to use my network to access investors to begin to design and build larger projects and become a full-time developer. It's fun, it has plenty of variety, and I certainly don't miss the commute into Liverpool Street...'

Staleness can hit a professional career at any time – but it doesn't need to signal the start of a long, slow decline. The key is to prepare for it, be honest about it when it happens to you, and have options for reinvention to hand. Doing nothing is a dangerous option.

KEY QUESTIONS

1. How full is your 'engagement' fuel tank?
2. What 'side hustle' could you begin to give more time to?
3. What are the opportunities for incremental change within your current role or organisation?

Your Optimise Action Plan

Pick **one** strategy from **each grouping** and commit to implementing every week for three months!

Mind

Reframe adversity into opportunity	☐
Track progress as well as results	☐
Find a safe place for critical reflection	☐
Be alert to wilful blindness	☐
Avoid pointless comparisons	☐
Manage your inner critic	☐
Identify a 'self-soothing' ritual	☐
Have a Plan B	☐

Body

Refresh to perform	☐
Get moving	☐
Eat smart	☐
Sort out sleep	☐

Relationships

Eliminate energy drains ☐
Put boundaries around 'keystone' relationships ☐
Get comfortable disappointing people ☐
Get feedback and adjust course ☐
Help other people – gain perspective ☐
Nurture the tribe ☐
Assemble 'Team You' and ask for their help ☐
Celebrate individual and collective achievement ☐

Acknowledgements

In addition to the people who are mentioned in the main text, the following individuals have been instrumental in helping me complete this book, so to them I send my gratitude:

Anjel Noorbhaksh, Gail Kinman, Joanna Page, John Callaghan, Louise Edwards, Matt Croucher GC, Shruti Ajitsaria, Sue Powell.

My daughters are always a special source of inspiration, so thanks to Jess and Freya.

And to Sarah, who has been my sounding board for so much of the content, love and thanks.

The Author

 Steven Pearce is a coach and consultant who helps professional advisers raise their game. Since 2005, he has helped thousands of professionals become more effective through individual and group coaching, workshops and keynote speeches. Based in the UK, he offers training and coaching in the Optimise system, both in-person and online.

Visit www.optimise-now.com for bonus interviews and materials, to take the Optimise self-assessment, and to join the Optimise community.

For all coaching and speaking enquiries, connect with Steven at:

- 🐦 @stevenjpearce
- 💼 linkedin.com/in/stevenjpearce
- ✉️ steve@optimise-now.com

Lightning Source UK Ltd.
Milton Keynes UK
UKHW020825181120
373623UK00009B/331